A DRAMATIC LIFE

HOW TO JOURNEY WITH ELEMENTARY THINKING

Kevin C. McCrewell, Sr.

outskirtspress

DENVER, COLORADO

Ashley, K.C., Allie and Sharon

*You can limit the drama, by eliminating
the elements of controversy.*

Table of Contents

Foreword..vii

Drama Described 1

Elementary Thinking 6

Drama Detective 11

Choosing Your Drama.................................14

Drama Reporter 19

The Myth, The Legend, Myself 24

The Drama Of Fear.....................................28

The Drama Of Sex 35

Diagnosis, Drama..41

The Price Of Drama....................................45

Dramatic Division.......................................49

Drama Phobia 56

Drama By Misdirection 59

The Drama Of Love....................................64

Dramatic With Pride 75

A Dramatic Return......................................81

Epilogue..87

FOREWORD

In the new millennium, the definition of a single word has changed. A word which in it's basic form, gives broad strokes to so much in it's new role in our lives ... DRAMA.

The word drama is now the descriptive catch-all for events, not even catastrophic. Events which can alter the course of a moment, day or even change one's life.

Throughout this book you will see instances of drama that may seem to be the same as another already listed. But, that's how drama is, coming around again unless you stop it.

To some of you, this may seem like a book about the negative things in life. Instead, use this as a way to look back, learn and even laugh at the peaks and valleys of life ... your life.

To some of you, this book won't make any sense. It will seem like a long rant about nothing. You will not understand how anyone could have such drama in their lives. How things so small and even trivial to you could lead to so much.

Yet for the rest of us, getting past drama is a daily struggle. Its damn hard work and we have all we can do not to get caught up in it.

We'll talk about Elementary Thinking and how a little thought can go so far to limit your personal drama. Remember, what you do sometimes in life not only affects self. Others may pay the price for the chances and choices you spend and squander.

This is about the most powerful force on earth. Something anyone can use without material cost. It's power so infinite, that whole continents can be changed by one person's use of it. Any disease can be cured by it and its imaginative power can create great things or transport it's user to different worlds.

It is the strength and power of thought that I speak of, brain power. It is will, desire that you as an individual can call upon. This is using your intellect to make a world for yourself and others.

It's so many of the little things that we start the day with, even some from yesterday. You must start clean without any baggage from the previous day, with a hot cup of positive outlook. You think nothing about a shower and or shave, brushing your teeth, styling your hair. So, why don't we use as much energy and thought to how we will travel through our new day?

From cutting your finger to an arrest by the police, everything has an elementary basis. The trick is to identify and avoid what can become controversial and lead to your own personal drama.

Part of my observations is based upon my interaction and observations of others, including family and friends. I have been married, have three great kids and try to keep an open mind. I have tried many ways to find new experiences. I guess I want to sample everything and otherwise I just have a great love of life. I'm still trying to enjoy new experiences and live each day as it comes, setting a goal for each and every day.

I am not a doctor, nor do I make any clinical claims. This book is about the author's view of life and my opinion is certainly not to be considered gospel. I write this as a catalyst for conversation and see it as a way of opening the door to proactive thinking.

This is a chance for my spirit to grow and your spirituality to be enhanced. This done with a new way of gathering clean energy that I catalyze, you produce and use. So, we give to and take from each other. We team up to make our world a better, stronger place. Our new, cleaner thinking place having a few small controversies and no drama.

This book is about taking the drama and eliminating how we got there, what it was that made circumstances gather into a storm of change. As we go, hopefully you will see how to break down events into elementary morsels. In your journey through life, there are ways to apply logic and ethics to place yourself outside of the drama.

The word drama has a large role and is otherwise the real foundation of this book. Drama is the new word for troubles or everyday problems we face. I will try to show you some dramatic situations and their resolution using Elementary Thinking.

Elementary Thinking is a concept driven simply by common sense and spelled out in basic terms. Elementary Thinking is not only for you, it's about conversation, too. Tell a friend or loved one, that there just might be another way to look at life and maybe even make some sense out of it.

Life has a concentric cyclic basis having the ability to have events come back which you can predict by your choices, good or bad.

From birth, we have a platform and a start, the clean bottom. We leave the oval of the womb (it's not squared off like a box or a rectangle) and begin our journey.

The `Circle of Life' is the stuff of which our existence is made and is steered toward our end, the light at the end of our journey. The brain power with Elementary Thinking is the shield, sword and compass to guide and protect you.

DRAMA DESCRIBED

The circumstances that you put yourself into and surround yourself with can play a major role in just allowing you to have a normal day or a drama filled one.

Remember, it doesn't take a really big mistake or event. Sometimes it only takes one or more bad choices to start a chain reaction into drama. Take a look at the following list. Be honest and see if a trait, action or inaction about you is on it. Don't be afraid to see it in writing. Now maybe you have that something tangible to hold in your hand. Have you ever had an itch on your back that you couldn't reach to scratch?

Do any of these look familiar? ...

- Non-productivity
- Procrastination
- Hypochondria
- Failure to prioritize
- Substance abuse
- Overeating
- Unsafe sex
- Overspending
- Too much credit

- Promiscuity
- Poor vehicle maintenance
- Self-loathing
- Bad dating habits
- Poor personal hygiene
- Divorce
- Too many tattoos or piercings
- Envy
- Bankruptcy
- Failure to take prescribed medications
- Smoking
- Inability to be monogamous
- No regular doctor visits
- Buying a fighting dog as a family pet
- Insomnia
- Sexual addiction
- Greed
- Unsafe recreational activities
- Rumormongering
- Overstating self verbally or in writing
- Fear
- Inappropriate conversation
- Improper/inappropriate fashion choices
- Impulsive behaviors
- Tardiness
- Adultery
- Failure to share emotions
- Selfish behavior
- No future planning
- Jealousy
- Bad investing
- Paranoia
- Poor personal conduct in the workplace

ELEMENTARY THINKING + YOU

SELF AWARENESS/SELF TRUTH
= BETTER LIFE POTENTIAL

That formula was pretty fancy ... Thank you. It really means be honest with yourself and not 'thin-skinned'. Look at the list as not absolute and totally preventable.

Show this chapter to a friend, lover or even just someone you know. I know I don't have everything listed, but I'll bet the list will make for some great conversation. You know something about you is listed and/ or recognizable about someone you know.

I'm sure you can come up with plenty more reasons why or how drama begins or just what drama means to you. I know I just barely scratched the surface, but try to recognize your own dramatic fire starter on the previous list or come up with one of your own. Then be proactive, attack it, slice it up into elements and let it blow away into the wind. There is a great deal of negative here, but you can't fight what you can't see. So, look around as we continue on our journey together.

Make your own list from your life and use elementary thinking to break down these events and see how you made your choices. Look at what you did with an open mind, show yourself honestly how to repair what you can. Avoid making the same mistakes twice, break the negative cycle.

You may never see these examples or descriptions in print again, but you know their effects are everywhere. Please add the drama list to the encyclopedia of life in the back of your brain. The list is a "cheat sheet" you can use to recognize trouble.

One you train your brain using Elementary Thinking, you will no longer see drama. You will be able to feel drama, and break controversies into little bits that never have a chance. Remember, if you put yourself on the right path for your journey through life, you will have less dramatic opportunities just by where you place yourself.

You don't have to be a prophet, just sound like one with the right mind set. Love yourself first as the base, proactive with thought using Elementary Thinking as your guide. With this type of self awareness and self truth added, you really just can't help but have better life potential.

Put out the drama fires, you can see them now. Build your drama reflexes to help you stay clear of the negative within and without your Circle of Life.

So, let's sum up after all of that. Drama is a large amount of negative or controversy, which can disrupt or wobble our Circle of Life. Elementary Thinking helps us to limit or prevent drama by helping us to make better choices. Make choices which keep problems at the solvable, controversial level, before they can accumulate into drama.

So much in our lives is cyclic, running in circles. Drama fits this so well, it will come right back to you if you do not remove dramatic problems completely.

Don't underestimate the power of drama and its ability to gather controversy and amplify it. Think of living from paycheck to paycheck and how even the smallest of changes to your budget can create chaos. Is putting a few bucks aside each week just in case Elementary Thinking? Would that car repair bill have been made easier to pay? Sure would help for that unexpected chaos spelled d-r-a-m-a.

ELEMENTAL THINKING

What is Elemental Thinking?
(Live well in the present, steer well into the future)

Elemental Thinking is vision. It's being able to see ahead of self while remaining grounded. In other words, use ethics and logic to build and lead yourself into a better and greater future.

Another way, think about what it is that you wish to accomplish each and every day of your life. As you wake, set into motion your plan for the day. Follow through, but be flexible and react with thought. Be proactive with thought about the final outcome as you go about your day.

Think of drama while using Elementary Thinking as... **D**etermined to **R**esurrect and **A**chieve to **M**end and **A**dvance.

Elemental Thinking is a lifestyle, a conscious way of living during which we break down events as we journey along the Circle of Life. Remember, this circle is really a tunnel with a light at the end of it. The question is how will you get to the light, how did you journey and is the end result at the light exactly what you wanted.

If you have religious beliefs, most faiths have a 'good book' describing philosophies and stories of how choices need to be made. These are based upon teachings described listing of what to and what not to do.

I know this is a book about drama and talking about religion is sure to bring that about. But, if you really look at the teachings of your religion or belief in a higher power, you can see the Elementary Thinking in 'the word'.

Religious teachings break everything down into elementary morsels, providing a full and detailed explanation. Cleansing of the body, mind and soul are listed throughout most books. I won't question the wisdom here, but writings thousands of years which have passed the test of time just might be correct.

What is avoidable potential for controversy? Don't the good books teach us to live clean lifestyles and to honor and love a higher power as well as self? What about being prepared?

These things written so long ago are as relevant today as they were then.

Ethics and a value set in government or the corporate world are spoken about frequently and often displayed as badges of courage or banners of self-advertisement.

*

Physical		Personal
	*	*
Love		Professional
	*	*
Spiritual		Family
	*	

- CIRCLE OF LIFE -

ELEMENTARY THINKING

Leaders   •   often times have the best 'vision'

           •   think outside of 'the box'

           •   follow through until the end

           •   set goals and strive to go beyond them

Followers •   have tunnel vision, never looking ahead

           •   only thinking of self and what's close to them

           •   procrastinate and/or defer to others

           •   live for today, never saving or preparing

Followers can't fight off dramatic events and they fall behind and the cyclic events drown them. This dragging down finally catches and stops the follower.

Leaders are looking, thinking and doing so far ahead using Elementary Thinking, drama can't catch up. Only a small amount of controversy will even be around to react to, brushed aside as daily life.

Ever hear of the term 'well rounded'? That's synonymous with being complete.

"Man, he's got it all together. He has a beautiful wife, home, good kids, great job, nice car, money in the bank." To most, being complete is the 'American Dream', that of success and some kind of wealth. But, wealth does not have to be monetary. Wealth can be so much more with the Circle of Life in mind.

Elementary Thinking and the Circle of Life go hand in hand. If you can keep the circle rolling smoothly by using Elementary Thinking, you will truly have wealth each and every day of your life.

The Circle of Life is a pathway through and to the end of your life. Remember, conscious choices by you affect others, so don't walk with blinders on.

The circle has six main parts which require constant adjustment each and every day. No day will ever be perfect, but a little controversy is much better than drama which is major.

The personal part of the circle starts with you. Remember, there are people who love you. So, don't forget to love yourself. Your actions affect those close to you especially.

Show everyone your personal power. This is done by being, not acting. When you walk the talk, you shine like a beacon. Being you is the only action needed here.

People will see your smile and be drawn to it. Positive energy is like a magnet, but beware of negative persons. They will attempt to steal your energy. You know, the supervisor that comes to work with a bad attitude and spends all day making your workplace a torture chamber.

True Elemental Thinkers know that a positive defense to negative energy is not to be thin skinned. You can't cure negative people, that cure comes from within all of us, within ourselves.

Remember, self-empowerment.

A good personal life depends on rest, nutrition, lifestyle choices, attitude and a willingness to be surrounded by less dramatic positive persons. It will take self-restraint, but you need to avoid negative people. You cannot cure them and often you will enable their negativity and make matters worse.

Next, your professional life needs attention too. Everyone knows that if you're not happy at work, you're not happy at home. Hypertension and other stress related disease and disorders, sexual dysfunction, substance abuse, chronic fatigue syndrome and a long list of other problems.

There is nothing worse than being in a job that is not suited for you and the stress which is synonymous with drama. If you think that your Circle of Life will roll straight, guess again.

Your personal life and family can be greatly affected by your poor career choice. Your misery will be borne by your friends and loved ones who empathize with you about your drama.

Your physical life will suffer, there will be little or no sex and your spiritual flame will be extinguished easily, because it does not burn as brightly as it used to.

You may have personal and professional problems which now poison your family life. Everyone has family, whether biological, social and/or emotional. This includes pets too, because they have feelings and they will interact and influence the family.

In a number of professions, the 'word' is don't take the job home with you. This means that the things you see and do are not what most can easily understand.

If your relationships are already entrenched, you will need to walk softly and allow your family to 'soak up' what you do. Keeping things to yourself is absolutely not the way to handle how your family deals with your professional life. Walking softly is not picking and choosing what to tell, it's how you tell it.

Internalizing, is taking in your work or professional problems and not finding an outlet for your stress and/or feelings. Going to a bar after work is not the way to heal after a long day.

Do you think that drama won't find you at a bar? Coming home after 'self-medicating' just smells bad, literally. This is no way to deal with your professional issues and your circle will wobble out of balance very quickly here. There can be an argument that takes place when you get home, and are the kids watching?

Spirit is our personal energy. It is what we are as people and as a people. Our interaction with others in life is a display of our spirit, our self. Spirituality is often defined as how we worship religiously, a higher being or consciousness.

Your spiritual life is any of these things and something I would like to add, attitude. What people see about you is often what you provide them to form opinions about.

For some, their spiritual selves or how they worship dictates their actions and or conduct throughout their Circle of Life. Often means not absolute because of prejudice, which does not allow for the experience or seeing of the spirit.

Spirituality fits on the circle between love and family, and with good reason. It could be said that spirit, love and family are a sub-circle in all of this. This is the true area of the circle that means the most to human beings, civilized or not.

Spiritual energy is much more than just something you believe in or your values. Remember, that because of love, your family will absorb some of this energy which also affects how they live and their spiritual display. This love energy can be like the glue that binds all together and can make you and yours invincible.

Now we have reached the physical, this is also who we are for all to see. Prejudice can play a large role here, so resist the urge to be 'thin-skinned'.

Body type or shape, height, hair color, skin color, muscularity, sound of your voice, and how you speak. Don't forget about these things, but they are not completely who you are. So don't dwell on the body, concentrate on the spirit. Spiritual energy is not only felt by you physically, but projected toward others. Positive thinking can lead to positive changes in your professional life, as well as less stress and better health of your physical being.

If you are unhappy, do you think it's easier to gain weight or just have an overall feeling of dread? It takes a conscious effort each and every day to maintain good health. Health or wellbeing is a way to move forward on our journey through life with less resistance.

Maintaining your physical being can lead to promotion and or opportunity. Can you do things better when you feel well? Don't people ask, are you o.k.? If you don't pay attention to how you look, can anyone see the real you or what you really are?

Family falls into the love and spiritual sub-circle. The foundation of the Circle of Life is our family. Family being the place we start the day at and the people we start the day with in our hearts and minds.

Our family is our legacy, our imprint on life. It's what we leave for others to see and it's what we create by who we are.

Remember, a family does not have to be large to be vital. It need be only you and that one special other to make a family.

I know I have yet to really talk about love and its role. I guess that's because of its power and impact. Love is a catalyst and can heal. It is hope, warmth and strength. Love is the glue that can bind our family together and give us courage to take life head on.

If you love your physical self and are truly comfortable about whom you are, you will 'glow' from the strength of your spirit. The strength of your spirit is that happy look, that constant smile which everyone is drawn to. Ever hear of a person's infectious smile or wit?

So much can be said for being in love. What speaks volumes is the love of life you can have and it's effect upon all aspects of your circle of life.

Armed with knowledge, drama should now be...

Develop a plan to break the negative circle/cycle

Realize you are human and can make mistakes

Admit when you make bad choices

Make changes and heal

Allow for positive change using Elementary Thinking

Elemental Thinking is vision, a way of life, almost like a form of spirituality. It's drama repellent, a conscious effort each and every day of your life to make anew and to renew self and influence others. Some of this can be done just by being you. Set a goal for each and every day of your life. This goal is yours and you can reach it with your initiative. If your spirit is clean, others will offer their energy and some will just be there to help.

Remember, Elemental Thinking is vision and being able to break down events subconsciously, avoiding controversies that can lead to drama. See the path ahead and avoid the trouble spots that will wobble your Circle of Life. See it, avoid it, and move forward positively.

Reach your daily goal and live well today. If you do not wake tomorrow, how would you judge the way you lived and want to be judged?

DRAMA DETECTIVE

Being reactive is setting the stage for your drama, a story that has a beginning and numerous bad endings.

Ignore the 'check engine' light and you will react by calling a tow truck to pick up your oil dripping, smoking vehicle. Stop the vehicle, check the fluids, and call the tow truck to save your engine. Don't continue on because you are close to your destination. The destruction of your engine is drama, so stopping your vehicle lessens the blow. But, replacing your engine and causing yourself a serious financial strain is unacceptable.

Reactivity is an element that is a response to your realization that controversy will result or has already begun.

Drama fits well into your life because your life is well suited to accept it. The question is do you have the value set and practice good ethics in order to succeed? Life is really a set of concentric circles, the cycles of the Zodiac, the moon, and menstruation. A wedding ring as a symbol of unbroken, unending love and so on. I like to think of life as a tunnel, an elongated circle with a light at the end of it. Our journey through life is to get to the light. What this light contains or is comprised of is the great question pondered by scholars over the decades, but still has no definitive answer. For our purposes, let's talk about this tunnel and how drama impacts our passage through it.

Getting to the light takes a lot of daily work. Each day you must set a goal or goals you need to reach to lessen or avoid drama. Folks, not every day can be a success. But, with enough effort, you can literally make a zone around yourself to allow for damage control.

Be a detective and find the dramatic clues that give your life that special touch. React to their potential, that's pro-activity. The clues or elements are yours from the day you are born and can be controlled.

Elementary Thinking takes the clues and solves life's riddle with proactive steps. The light at the end of the tunnel of life, is really only finding some kind of peace. The light is inner joy, heaven within self.

The light is coming home and finding food in the pantry. The kids have clothes and are healthy. The bills are paid past the next payday and are all up to date. Your parents are well; one of your co-workers just told everyone he beat his cancer.

It doesn't take all of those things, maybe just some or one. The light is the ability to illuminate drama, see problems (pro-activity) and move them out of the way with slight course changes (reactivity).

Can't this light be experienced prior to death? How about being enlightened while living? Can this light be your own heaven on earth? To be truly happy, find or detect your drama starters and avoid reactivity.

At some point, your life starts to run on auto-pilot. When this happens, it will be tough to find drama in your life. Don't forget to be thankful for the peace and healing you find and can give to yourself and those around you.

Keep an ever watchful eye on you and yours, the dramatic clues will be there. Will you be able to analyze them and avoid them? Or, will you just be another drama detective who sees the problem, but does not have a clue on how to find a solution.

Cyclic interpretation is keeping your life rolling smoothly using Elementary Thinking. This is the vision that I speak of. Is it really actual sight or is it a feeling or a lifestyle. It's really all of those things and more. It's "can you see what I'm saying?"

Dramatic detection is not really seeing, it's feeling. It's not looking at things with a microscope, it's a course of action taken in response to recognized negative energy that you perceive or detect as you go through your daily routine. It's also an ever present shield that you develop using Elementary Thinking.

You can feel the warm glow of seeing the light ahead, even having it all around you. Isn't the term 'seeing the light' synonymous with understanding? It's not psychic interpretation; it's applying a reason-ableness test to yourself and those around you. Application of this test is either proactive or reactive thinking, depending on when you use it.

It's about better choices, decisions that steer you down the right path. Choices that avoid the pothole filled path along life's journey. Remember what Sherlock Holmes used to say, "It's elementary..." He solved dramatic problems by just taking a little extra time to look around and really see. Taking the time to look at the pieces and come up with a sum based on those parts. Can you?

CHOOSING YOUR DRAMA

Do we need to talk about non-productivity? It's one thing not to be able to make your machine due to a lack of parts from the other division. But can't you speak to your manager about the slow down?

This is drama that you can reason with by using Elementary Thinking to find the way around what is problematic here. Here you don't have to cause the problem yourself as illustrated, but you do have to come up with a solution. Ultimately your non-productivity will be highlighted and your lack of problem solving will hold you back. Now, were you proactive or reactive here? Elementary Thinking always says be proactive to prevent drama before it starts.

That expense report has a due date. When submitted, a check is sent to you as a reimbursement for the monies spent on behalf of the company throughout the period. So, why is it late? When some of your payments are past due and you literally have money sitting on your desk, who is really to blame here? Do you blame your creditors, your job or just yours truly?

Procrastination is another workplace fire starter and is merely waiting for the other shoe to drop. Doing this, you are allowing some person or event to move in and affect you without response, putting off what you really need to do.

Why wait until the last day of college class registration and then complain because the class you need or wanted is full? Partying or sleeping in were the best choices then, but won't the really great times be paid for with that degree later? Remember that Friday exam last year? You knew it was only Tuesday. Why study when you could go to that meeting and gathering on Wednesday and that party on Thursday. Now, it's Friday morning, time to study. Wait for the exam results ... DRAMA!

Put off the important things, they can wait. "I was supposed to meet my boyfriend at eight. But my girlfriend called and we stopped for a drink after work." When you are late and he's so angry that he doesn't return your calls, why do you question his love for you?

Using Elementary Thinking you can see that professionally you suffer by the obvious possible loss of employment or status in the workplace. You can't get that job without education which is self-enrichment of a highly personal and professional nature. Can you feed your family with your non-bonus due to your lack of productivity? How long will your spirits soar with the loss of that relationship? Was it due to your lack of being able to prioritize? As your love life fades here, so does your ability to positively affect your overall wellbeing. You know that neck ache is really concentrated tension. The lack of sleep is due to worry; the oversleeping is due to low self-esteem. Now your family and friends start to notice changes, you become depressed, never really smiling anymore. You're on edge at home and at work.

See a circle starting, a circle created by a choice you made or allowed someone to make for you. Don't be surprised when this choice comes back around to set you off if you do not react pro-actively in response.

I remember one day while in flight school, I was on a final approach to land. Nearby, some parachute jumpers were landing in an area just off of the runway. My instructor said, "Look at those meat missiles. Why jump out of a perfectly good aircraft?"

I really didn't know that Mark was a philosopher, but he certainly had guts being my flight instructor.

Flying aircraft can be a safe and rewarding hobby or even profession. But what about flying hang gliders or balloons, parachute jumping, bungee jumping, playing 'chicken' with cars, 'Russian Roulette', street car racing, excessive drinking games, base jumping, backyard wrestling, mountain or rock climbing. Running with the bulls?

Elementary Thinking here says living is risky enough, so why increase odds or tip scales towards drama. It's the rush of knowing you're a heartbeat away from your demise, right?

I guess some just want to get to the white light at the end of life's journey faster than others. I guess you can't experience drama if you're dead. But isn't an untimely death drama too?

Now you know that the drug test you are about to take is going to get you that great job. So why did you smoke marijuana at the card game last night? Which was more important, living for the 'get high' today or years of work towards a pension and great pay with benefits?

REALITY CHECK!

If you think that extra squirt of perfume is not noticed, it is. That sour smelling shirt … if it smells a little to you, it smells a lot to someone else. You need to look at your choices (Elementary Thinking?) and make the hard decisions as you start your day. Pheromones are one thing; we do not overtly detect them. Your body odor is not an ocean summer breeze. Elementary Thinking says that a little soap, water and a toothbrush go a long way.

Do we really need to go further into this? The rule of thumb is … if it has a little odor or is just o.k. to you, it's probably not.

Folks, let's just tell it like it is. Staring at your attractive to you coworkers is not cool. Crying on the phone on company time because of a conversation with your significant other is not cool either. Did you slam your hand down on your desk in frustration? How about repeatedly sniffling or snorting? Do you have the cough that won't stop? Are you passing gas when you think no one can smell or hear you?

Personal space is extended up three feet from self. Now knowing this, why would you even reach out and touch someone. Better yet, why would you reach out and touch someone inappropriately in the workplace, threatening your future professional standing, livelihood and maybe even landing you in jail.

"Oh but he's cute and the kids love him." Let's keep this simple. A gun can be shiny and really look like a fine piece of art. Load it and put it into someone's hands and drama can and will result. So why buy a fighting dog as a family pet? How many times have you heard stories about Pit Bull and other fighting terriers biting, maiming and killing people? Are these animals used as protection or as cover?

Can we find protection from our bad choices as a result of non-elementary thinking or as cover from their negative consequences? Think before you leap, your grandmother used to say. So why don't you make a dramatic choice to stop or protect yourself from drama?

Machines need to be fed like we do. Electricity, oil, gasoline and more is the nourishment. Everyone needs a vehicle in order to get through life, so why not take care of your investment. No oil changes, blown engine. Bald tires, slide into another vehicle. Insurance rates go up, your vehicle needs to be repaired, you're injured or they are and they file suit. Lose time at work; put your professional standing in jeopardy. One thing will lead to another, in a circle.

In certain settings, tattoos and piercings can be badges of courage or even sexy. But folks, grow up and realize that we still deal with copious amounts of racism and other forms of discrimination and or prejudice our society. People with tattoos and piercings are often seen as rough or angry from another culture. Pierced lips, eyebrows and noses are uncommon and look uncomfortable or even painful. Ever look away from the television because something appears to be intensely unattractive or painful?

Tattooing or body art may be a statement of rebellion or even an expression of your inner self. But don't expect a deviation from conservative values to accommodate your need for self-expression. In some cultures, tattoos are a desecration of the flesh. Think of 'vivid' tattooing or piercings as a desecration of your social status or professional life if they can't be covered easily.

The choices or decisions we make can be dramatic, explosive and destructive. At some point you need to check and see if you are really ready to cash the drama paycheck you have written for yourself.

If you are going to choose an effort to risk your life and or wellbeing, take a moment to run through several negative outcomes in your mind as examples. Take the worst case scenario and apply it to several of your choices before you start out. I guess if you wince or get a chill, that choice is out.

So much simple common sense can apply here. Our lives are fast enough, take a moment and give yourself time to make a better choice. No choice is ever set in stone. Even with the right choice, luck or random chance can lend a negative hand here. But, by taking the time to make an informed decision, it will certainly give you better odds.

To sum it up, Elementary Thinking says think first and make better choices. Remember, until you become President, others will control how your life goes. Will you be able to influence the course of your life? By making better choices you can self-empower and steal their thunder.

Not being controversial as a way of life, is how to best survive in the new millennium. Try tuning values to steer towards better choices and ultimately a non-dramatic result. It's about choosing the right path and or lifestyle to avoid negative energy or events, also known as drama.

DRAMA REPORTER

In life, I have seen a great many things and I hope many more. During this life, I have known the destructive power of the drama reporter, feeling the sting of their poisonous bite. This person thrives on presentation of another person's problems, almost stimulated or delighted by the froth created by the disclosure.

The drama reporter will expose any truths or untruths and no subject is off limits. To them, everything and anything about you or others is fair game.

This person is much worse than the misdirector, who wants out of the spotlight. Once out of the spotlight, they should be at ease that they are no longer the focal point, hidden from view. The drama reporter thinks that he or she is elevating their social status, gaining power and acceptance through the reporting of the misfortunes of others.

The drama reporter is always within earshot of the meeting in the office and they are ready and eager to furnish the details at its conclusion. They get in the middle of the conversation when the coffee truck comes and during the lunch break. They bring a foul property into a gathering of persons. This, I guess, is supposed to make them look like better people. But guess what? While all the reporting is going on, the reporter is getting caught in the spinning of the tales and is not seeing that the drama tales are really drawing negative attention to themselves. I guess just draw a big bull's-eye on your own back and just wait to feel the stab.

Rumormongering is full scale drama reporting and often is just dramatic misdirecting. I like to use the person who spreads rumors as a vehicle to get my message to the masses. You know, telling the right person that you don't like something your employees are doing.

As the story goes, if you have nothing good to say, then say nothing at all. Drama is both glue and a boomerang when rumormongering. As you spit evil with your forked tongue, expect someone to tie you to what is said. Even if you are just passing along what you hear, expect it to boomerang back to you. And, the friend or colleague that was the subject of the drama is going to come to you for answers. Now many new names will be stuck to you like glue because you didn't use Elementary thinking, realizing the consequences and avoid the dramatic result.

Sometimes when I write this, I feel like I'm stating much more than the painfully obvious to a fault. Yet, we still have to hear such foolish things said which just have no (expletive!) class. Those things presented can be just far beyond shocking. So bad, you wonder how a person could even have a brain to make up the words.

O.k. so, here goes...

Ever hear at a wedding about how sexy the bride is and how the story teller dated her, way back when? A bunch of guys are at the loading dock and an attractive blond in a mini-skirt and heels, walks up holding a lunch bag. You say, "Oh my god she's hot. I want her naked now!" As you finish, her husband who is waiting for his lunch reaches out and punches you in the face.

At the wake, someone always has to bring up how the deceased was good, but they drank or smoked too much. Or the infamous comparison with other funerals and wakes they attended. Oh, let's not forget talking bad about relatives instead of a positive focus on the good things about the deceased. Oh by the way, you can't look so good if you're dead.

Make up some of your own stories here, it's easy. Elemental Thinking says consider where you are and who you are with before opening your BIG mouth!

Using Elementary Thinking, one would have to think that if one did not cast other people in a negative light, then perhaps they could be supported by other people because they are not associated with anything negative. Now I know this is too closely aligned with common sense, but you will never see this with blinders on. Use the big picture as your guide, along with a better value set for clarity.

Drama is a poison and common sense is the only antidote. Remember, Elementary Thinking breaks down drama into avoidable potential for controversy. Setting the course (values) and steering away from these avoidable controversies (value system), can limit or eliminate the dramatic result. Taking complete charge and responsibility of self can lead to inner strength and peace. Be yourself, you are the only one like you. That makes you a rare and valuable commodity.

Too much information or T.M.I. needs to apply here ... sexual prowess described, kissing and telling. Don't forget descriptions of imaginary kissing and still telling.

I don't know about you, but the level of disgust in regards to people who divulge the details of intimate acts goes well beyond what I could easily describe. When involved in intimacy, a level of trust is automatically created by human nature. Yet, there are some which are stimulated by the telling of their sexual tales. These are tales which repel others with great force.

Frankly, if I had a fantasy, I would have sex and the time to have it, twice daily. So, I guess this would require me to put a white circle on the back of my car and the number two with an x. So, that means I like sex twice daily. I wonder if I put silhouettes of people in my favorite intercourse positions on my car's bumper is too much.

Is this too much information?

Elemental Thinking says if you can't show it or do it in public, then you know it should be kept private. An open door policy with your sexuality will bring you drama. I'm not trying to tell you how or with whom you have sex with. But, as in everything else, prejudice will follow you if you let it.

You can't practice Elemental Thinking if you are telling people that you are gay or lesbian and wearing it on your sleeve. Your sexual orientation is not a badge of courage. It's just too much information to display, it's an invitation for people to look at your car and visualize you having sex. Frankly, I don't need the distraction about your sexual preferences. Enjoy yourselves behind closed doors and often. In relationships, be as demonstrative as you need to be. Be in love; give love and hold on to it and your partner. Anyone and everyone should be able to see your partner, your choice. No one needs to see your intimate sexual preferences.

It's not about what you do or who you do it with. The drama is in the 'in your face' attitude. Pushing and or forcing something upon others will be a negative force, and don't act like the victim when someone negatively responds to your display.

Keeping it simple, some stories are best left unsaid. It can't bring you drama if it's not there. Just because you are proud does not mean you will be understood by all. So, be proactive with your releases of the most intimate details of your life and how you live it. The potential for drama is there, pro-act don't react to it.

We all know what we want for ourselves and who we want to be. So, I don't think an advertisement of self will bring about any great change. It's about your positive energy, shielding yourself and empowering others.

Your political choices are as volatile as your lifestyle choices. The candidates you choose prior to an election or how you feel about our leaders can affect perception of self. Again, it's not about freedom of speech, the cornerstone of our country. It's about the potential for drama to take hold and blur perception. You may make an intelligent choice, but should you rely on the media or intellect of others to see it clearly?

Too many times, I have allowed people to take how I lived my life at their face value. If I had used Elementary Thinking as a young man,

I would have realized early the good person inside. The good person will be there and only persons smart enough will see this, the rest will not benefit.

Think about how much time you spend trying to look your best. Remember to concentrate on who you are and especially who you are not. This is not to say you can't be more, but you must be yourself and not the vision of someone else.

So, dramatic reporting can be vocal or visual, implied or just in your face. The trick is to realize where and when to be on display, or to just sit back and watch the fireworks. Your power is who you are, what you know and feel. Power is not how you project yourself or plead your case.

Hold on to your power, yourself and hold it tightly. Do not expect others to understand you. Remember that others are looking for the same things you are, so share your power by being proactive in thought. Don't expect your power to be noticed, but don't you have to live with yourself?

THE MYTH, THE LEGEND,

MYSELF

In life, there are contenders and pretenders. The contenders are the average Joe's and Jill's of the world who go through daily life, taking each day as it comes. These are ordinary people with grounded behaviors and sense of self. These are the people of self-restraint and assessment, knowing one's limitations in financial and social situations. If this is you, congratulations you can have a normal life. Of course you need to watch out for drama each and every day. You might even have a long and fruitful life.

However, there are those who cannot deal with just being ordinary humans. These are true legends in their own minds and they thrive on their own self-created aura.

One day you'll be standing next to one of those legends. They will introduce themselves and seem very polite and even friendly. But, get to know them and the drama begins.

Two men will be standing next to each other, as a muscle-bound man walks by. One says to the other, "he is way too big for me to take him". The other says, "I can take him, I was a Navy Seal". Now we all know that Navy Seals, Green Berets and the like want to be out of the limelight, active or not. However, the drama of being more important than someone else far outweighs the need for restraint. The real drama begins when a real 'Seal' or loved one of someone who served confronts the pretender. Any number of negative emotions can surface, now that is real drama.

Imagine that this pretender represents his or herself as having technical prowess, like being in the medical field. They talk a great game, some even finding a way to practice their imaginary craft.

Enter your loved one at a time of crisis. You are now depending on the lifesaving training and ability of this 'expert' and they console you after their best effort has failed. There were elements that you missed, did you see them? Didn't you notice that the school diplomas on the wall were copies? What about the look of the office, it had a cheap feel to it now didn't it? The person took charge and appeared to use the right terminology, but the person did not appear to have enough help.

Why is it that whenever anyone wants to be more than they really are, they describe themselves as former police officers, medical professionals or soldiers? The best help you can give here is to literally walk away from this dramatic performance. It's really the only way to stop it. Take away the stage and there is no place to give the show.

Elementary Thinking suggests that honesty is a great platform for major gains like respect and trust. Remember the old phrase; what you see is what you get? People get to understand the real you and you can be your natural self, instead of a dramatic player in a bad life play.

In order to contend, you must be ready to defend against the drama traps set for you. Our issues do not have to be that large or vivid in order to enlarge or magnify a negative result into drama.

If you really want to test Elementary Thinking, go to any place where people gather and that serves alcohol. As the liquid courage flows, so do the stories of a greater or better self. As closing time approaches, the coupling urge throws reason and truth away. Mix alcohol with the emotions of finding out the truth on the next day...DRAMA!

In this information age, overstating the obvious can lead to major drama.

If the question on the application asks, 'did you graduate?' Answer, 'no' if you didn't. Why go through the hiring process, wasting the time and energy of many. What about the people you told about the good you have achieved for yourself. Describing an achievement or gain that was acquired by misrepresentation... D - R - A - M - A!

You must believe that by falsely making more of yourself, especially career wise, will result in your failure. Drama here takes many forms, arrest in some cases when applying for government employment or other benefit. Computer records can literally be a 'catch all' here and all misrepresentations will be exposed sooner or later.

Remember the story about 'The Emperor's New Clothes'? The emperor in his vanity thought he could be someone else, special in his new look. But, wasn't he the dramatic one. His need to be more than just himself led him down a path stripped of his ability to shield himself from drama. This path is an opportunity for you to be subject to ridicule and revenge. Was this emperor so vain, that he was blinded? Or was this a wealthy and powerful person, without enrichment?

Elemental Thinking could have stopped what his vanity started by just his deciding to lead without putting on the leaders robes. Get the take charge energy you need from within yourself. Thinking before you speak makes your words effective. Walking the talk is proof that you can lead by example.

Because of the emperor's demonstrated poor leadership and vanity, he drew anger and resentment (elements of controversy) which led to his embarrassing new invisible clothes.

Which do you think is more dangerous in a crowded room? Is it the person sitting quietly in the corner? Or the person in the center of the room, telling a joke to everyone as they intently listen?

Legends are made and talked about, not talked about and made. You can be so much more by spending more time sitting in the corner and listening, watching what's going on and learning about the crowd. While the joke teller was trying to be the center of attention, you were noticing what people were wearing, body language and other small things to help you. This information you used to help make it easier to meet and greet someone new in the crowd.

This chapter is all about how you draw drama to yourself like a magnet. As you keep reading this book, you will see the same dramatic problems come back around, often for different reasons. Believe that if you put out ten pounds of negative energy, expect at least ten or more back. Drama will cycle back to you if you let it.

Believe me, our society is so visually stimulated, perception and prejudice are only a glance away. Project an Elemental Thinker's view, positive energy and overall look. Be prepared, you will be a magnet which all will draw to and upon with great desire.

THE DRAMA OF FEAR

Few emotions in life cause us to resort to the most primal of actions. Self-preservation is king in moments of stress with no apparent remedy except your losing something.

Fear is stronger than love and the pain response. It is greater than family bonds and will cover a friendship with a dark cloak. The drama here is way too obvious.

Fear is like nitroglycerin, if you move or even lightly touch it … DRAMA! The fear of others has led to wars resulting in the deaths of millions. Were the Caesars' paranoid? How about Napoleon?

Even the smallest of transgressions (you know, bad actions) will bring about fear. Tell a baby "don't touch that!" The baby stops, looks at you and moves on. That baby practiced Elementary Thinking – it weighed the benefit to itself by touching the item. When the baby saw that mommy was mad, it moved away to avoid drama.

So what? Mommy was mad. But, Mommy might hit and we know we don't want her to yell at us. I know this baby example is incredibly simplistic, but it's the power of fear that affects this baby. A baby does not have the maturity to be influenced by anything that would cloak fear and allow it to defy what is really best.

Nature has given us a gift so profound to preserve self. Without this gift, we would probably self-destruct, each and every one of us. In addition, this gift will affect how we treat others, causing us to draft treaties with other nations in regards this gift to motivate. The gift is the pain response, a huge component of fear. It helps us know our limitations physically and emotionally as individuals.

Pain has a way of getting you through Elementary Thinking very quickly. It's really amazing how fast you can come up with ideas for eliminating your or your loved one's pain. Pain is pure drama and will blind your Elemental Thinking even past fear. But, remember there are those who will not manage their pain out of fear. These people will allow their pain to overwhelm themselves, often causing a greater problem than the one they should have initially dealt with.

Ever feel like you were being watched? Well, how about taking the lack of trust in others to the extreme. I guess you can never be too cautious, right? You know, spraying the phone after your aunt uses it at your apartment. Your little cousin sneaks up and takes a lick on your ice cream cone, so you throw it away. Your Dad says "here is some cash" and gives you a hundred dollars. You ask him so many times. "Are you sure? You don't need it?"

OVERKILL!

Envy is the capitalist catalyst. Do you think that's more than what's necessary for a description? Well, don't we all want to be better in some way, shape or form? A better job or more money would be good. Now why do we want the 'cool' car, the beautiful significant other, the big house, larger breasts and six-pack abs? Is it because we really need it or is what we see more desirable than our present condition? Envy is the cornerstone of capitalism, so is ambition.

How much is really enough of anything and how much is too much?

In a capitalist society like ours, the accumulation of wealth is envied and gives one power. What is the trigger which says that you should give back, share the wealth? I guess you earned it, right? So why share, don't you need more? I guess you can't be too careful.

Elementary Thinking is your conscience and belief on how you wish to be judged as a person, in this life and the next. The old saying about looking in the mirror at yourself really applies here. Some get so caught up in the excesses of their physical or spiritual wealth, that they forget where they came from. They forget the long dramatic road they took to get to today.

The fear of pain and the pain from fear is depression. Depression is like walking around with mirrored glasses, only the mirrors are on the inside. All you can see is yourself and all you see is how you look. You don't see how the look of your outer self affects your circle of life and blocks the view of your inner self. No longer having vision, you cannot move forward and drama is your only friend.

Depression is an anchor, a heavy one that you must drag with you everywhere you go. It's a physical and emotional 'black hole' that wobbles your circle of life by taking the emotional energy from yourself and others.

Sadness is a valley along the path of life and is as natural as the happy hills along the way. Relationship break ups, loss of a loved one or friend. If you have a fire or even a theft of belongings, things can go bad, negative things can happen to anyone.

Don't confuse sadness with depression. Sadness is a natural consequence of life. Take it head on and work through it with a natural affect. Don't try to mask it, let it flow through you and use what love you have inside as an aid in healing. This is in an effort to put a dramatic event that is in the present, into your past.

Depression is taking a glass filled with fear and drinking it down, dramatic liquid. This liquid stays inside you and won't go away until you release it. You and only you can ultimately take charge of your own fear. Even if it requires asking for help, the request must come from you.

Your circle of life requires daily maintenance, interaction with loved ones, going to work and play with good health and personal hygiene. If you are stuck in one place in your mind, how can you maintain your human condition or self? Your circle will wobble with controversy as others react to your new self.

Work will become more difficult due to lack of focus. Relationships will be strained as you lose sight of the people you need and their need of you. Self-medication is readily available to lessen the pain and this is a drama magnet, an easy fix to mask fear.

Pain is the food which depression lives on. Depression has a large appetite and is thirsty for positive energy. It will punch a hole in your circle of life, a hole which will swallow up anything you have tried to gain or anything you have.

Ever wonder why the very poor have so many children? If you can, imagine yourself in a living situation of darkness. The streets where you live are dirty, in need of repair. Trash and disrepair are found in the most common spaces. The area feels like a place where people are forgotten. Many families have one major parent figure and wealth is a hope based on a lottery ticket purchased with money you don't have.

Jobs are as scarce as education; entertainment is what passes by your open window on the street or sidewalk. Stress is everywhere here, counted on the number of legs used by the creatures which crawl in the walls of your apartment or from them. Opportunity is often what you take from each other. Tunnel vision is how you see today.

There is one free medication here, stolen moments which require no thought. For a few moments, a short time, life here can disappear. A brief coupling can make it all go away. A man can be a strong king or a hero. A woman can be a queen or a beautiful princess.

This self-medication costs nothing to have and cannot be taxed or stopped. No Elementary Thinking here, just a rinse away of the things that you dragged behind you. You gave yourself a quick chance at glory, a short time away from time.

For some, it is easier to react here. A negative mind set leaves no room for options. For others, creating a new life is what they think they are doing, but for whom? Some feel that this is how to make things right by showing others how. But, what is the real cost?

Here is the hardest place to find Elementary Thinking. There are the voices of many different countries and cultures, all trying to be heard. Many are trying to find a better place, but it is easier to take the free or cheap self-medication.

Empty time is another which leaves too many choices and not enough decisions. Gazing at an empty home or remembering the things you should have said, the things you should have done. You had your power then, but what about now?

Please take what I say here to heart. If yours is cold, chisel this into that mean dark cave in your chest. The elderly have too much time on their hands. Especially relatives, they need you. But, you do not have to be elderly to realize that you are alone. Picking up the telephone can be difficult, but can be as healing as any magic powder.

There is no drug that can cure you, no medicine that can erase the past or transport you to a better place. You cannot get a shot in the arm to make the world look peaceful or days seem brighter. There is no special drink to make you young or a magic spell to give you love and happiness.

There are many ways to excuse yourself from responsibility for what ails you. It's too easy to procrastinate or even give in to feeling sorry for yourself. It takes work to survive and only you can realize, stop and methodically heal you. But, the self-medication trap is nearby, caution!

Drama here can come in the form of drug use and or addiction, anti-social behavior or aggression. You can fall into domestic violence or abuse, reckless acts or even suicide. The drama is not limited to my examples and believe it or not, can include any combination or all of them.

Chemical imbalance either inherited or not, can be a factor. But, I'm talking about allowing choices to create so much controversy, that drama will result. That result, will cause fear of others or self. The pain of realizing that mistakes were made as hindsight takes over.

Elemental Thinking has to come into play here.

Draw upon the power of the energy given to you in your circle of life, ask for help and/or forgiveness. Take small steps to regain your power and begin to move forward again.

Don't forget what brought you down, depressing or pushing you below the path. Push off from it and climb back slowly. Be slow and deliberate, not fast and reckless. Heal by admitting your error and move on, change the negative channel.

Remember, the best medicine is self-empowerment. Push yourself every day to start well using Elementary Thinking. Keep your circle of life clear of the sickness of drama. Wellness really begins inside all of us. Make the effort to be well as a choice in life. Live each and every day as if it was your last, cherish each and every one.

No amount of wealth can protect you from an unhappy ending. Nothing will fall from the sky to change what you have done to be you. Only you can be you and to create who you really are to become.

The examples I give here are of situational depression or sadness due to external stimulus. You know, seeing bad stuff. These are things that effect how you deal with others and your life in general. As I stated earlier and I repeat now, only you can reverse this drama. Ultimately, you must decide that you need help. You must realize that your loved one or others must be trusted in what they see about you. You have to reach out and allow for intervention. Don't be afraid to realize you are not perfect and allow help to make you better. Don't be afraid to be medically evaluated.

Risk is opening up yourself or who you are, to external evaluation. Growth will be found with the help you get, you allow.

Self-empowerment can often be best accomplished with the help of others, unlock the doors and let the drama out and the help in.

As humans, fear has so many layers to hide beneath and many to hide from. Too much fear can be all consuming, not allowing for the experience of daily life. Too little breeds a reckless attitude and loss of focus on how important you really are.

Culture shock is a society's fear of change. Growth as a people will require something to change as they move forward. You will need to change as you move forward as a person. The human existence is fragile, easily damaged by self or others. You are not alone on this planet and there are many traps set for you and rivers to cross. Change is constantly going around you. Fear is not embracing change with pro-active thought about the good and bad while moving forward. Reactive thought says don't change until you have to. As you react, you play catch up and spend too much energy to get current.

Elementary Thinking says reactive catching up takes more energy than a simple proactive update. Fear is safe and does not require any intelligent effort by you at all. Change requires caution as you move forward past fear.

Do not be afraid of the future, its tomorrow and you can't stop it. You can change it with the choices you make today, steering toward the light at the end of your journey through the tunnel of life.

THE DRAMA OF SEX

Clearly as you read through our journey together, you can see that metaphors are grains of sand on this beach of a book. Sexual addiction is the greatest, most powerful and addictive 'drug' known to the human condition.

Did you notice that I said nothing about value or a price? Elementary thinking has big trouble here. Arousal and desire have a cloaking effect, covering our eyes like a blindfold.

Imagine yourself consumed by the need to have sex and without restraint. The extreme desire to perform the act, the strong need for the orgasmic release is intensified. Either alone or with someone, no age or gender is taboo. Bestiality, necrophilia, pedophilia, rape and incest are the extreme manifestations of this need.

For many, some definitions of what sex even is, needs to be put on a billboard to be seen and understood. Taboos and denial of something so personal can distort perception or just make us ignore what is right.

Let's start with the basics. The act of self-stimulation or masturbation is sex. Using your mouth to stimulate someone is sex, folks. Using fingers to stimulate up to and including penetration is sex, folks. Tongue kissing, the infamous back rub or foot massage, starting the process, foreplay.

The elementary rule is if you're stimulating or stimulated, it's probably sexual in nature.

Now, here's where the drama comes in … If addicted, you will be driven by your desire only and won't be thinking. Often, you will add intoxicants like alcohol and presto, you're having sex with someone. We all know about the car sex, club sex, exhibitionist sex, the quick feel when we think no one is looking. Ever go where you should not have because alcohol lowered your standards? Don't be a hypocrite; you know what is meant here.

The moment seems so right and passion overwhelms the two of you. Later, she may say it's your fault for not wearing a condom, but why didn't she use contraception? Both adults making a decision that will not last long, but could last a lifetime. Then who is to really pay for the unwanted pregnancy? Should the man bear all the cost? Or was an S.T.D. the result? No getting away from that, everyone pays and sometimes for life, too. How long would it have taken to stop at that gas station and pick up a condom?

Sometimes one's behavior can be influenced by another and this can influence other behaviors as well. Promiscuity, just seizing the sexual moment might feel great for that moment. But all kinds of drama can result. Sleep with someone who equates the act of sexual intimacy with value or sharing one's self. They take offense to your lack of realization that they just shared part of themselves with you out of friendship or even love.

Your act of recreation can lead to anger. Think of promiscuity as a game of chance, with the stakes being very high … yourself and your life.

Finding anger, S.T.D.'s, or degradation of self-esteem, can be perceived incorrectly by others. How about just not being able to form a lasting relationship because you have trained yourself to be safe.

For moral and health reasons, it would be best for everyone to have just one partner. That was the elementary, safe sex, common sense, socially acceptable, non-dramatic version we were told as children.

But you want to be a player, don't you? Tell your partners that you love them so that they will share themselves freely and openly, while you treat their emotional gift like everyday currency.

Anytime you bring others into your immediate and intimate space for friendship, business or love, you have a responsibility to act with respect and dignity.

To some, sex is never really love. It's like a transaction. I got what I needed and I picked you, hope you're satisfied. That person doesn't even realize that they may have changed your perception on the intimacy of sex and what love is or isn't. I have heard the stories about how they weren't monogamous because the other partner had no expectations of being in any type of relationship.

Elementary Thinking says emotions are like a match and drama is the dynamite!

Elementary Thinking might help prevent the finality of divorce, but we all should realize that this is the ultimate expression of a relationship failure. The drama here comes in so many intense forms, the scope of which is far reaching and lasting in effect. There are no winners, only pain for all involved and even more so for families with children.

TREAD LIGHTLY HERE. THIS SUBJECT OR EVENT CAN START EMOTIONAL EVENTS OF AN EXPLOSIVE NATURE – MUCH LIKE YOUR OWN PERSONAL 'WORLD WAR'. DIVORCE CAN INVOLVE MANY PLAYERS WHO DON'T KNOW YOU BUT CAN CONTROL YOUR LIFE, LEADING TO WAY TOO MUCH DRAMA!

Masturbation for the sake of release is often very therapeutic. However, the prolonged use of mechanical stimulation as an intimacy replacement can lessen the sexual response and add drama to something that's supposed to feel good naturally. Buying 'toys' with vibrations and pulsations that could never be replicated by any living human being, is a terrible mistake. The more simplistic the toy is, saves the human response when coupling. Drama will result when that moment comes when your partner brings you to plateau, but can't take you over the edge and into climax. Your partner is the same person physically that you met and fell in love with. But, now your appetite for sex and the orgasmic release have been self-adjusted to the point of your lessening of the intensity between you and your lover when together.

Make an effort to use less symbolism or mechanical stimulation when masturbating. The relationship you save may be your own. Remember, your partner will be very emotional about their inability to please you. Allow them to express their love for you and further bond with your lover as your body responds in hungry need and absorbs the moment's natural passion.

The sexual response is power just begging to be abused. Sex can be used to manipulate or even injure another. Sex, or the implied association, can sell a number of goods and services as well. Let's talk about some of the most common uses and misuses of the powerful and infectious sexual response.

Watch television commercials and you will find a commentary on how we think and feel as humans. We often see women in lingerie on our television screens with sexy music in the background, the male response of fantasy and a woman's response of seduction and beauty. Cars, beer, clothes, hair replacement, weight loss remedies, hygiene products and the list goes on of ways to sell, to entice using sex.

Playing to sex is not absent from politics and as we well know, our professional lives. We envy the young virile executive or the beautiful manager who gets promoted. There will always be someone who says that you got ahead because of how you look instead of how intelligent you are.

Using sex as fuel in your journey through life creates a pool of controversy just waiting for the strike of a match into dramatic fire. Sex is linked to such primal instincts, none of which is thought based. Pheromones, body curvature, eye and hair color included in the mix. Maybe, if you use a little extra attention verbally. Or, the slight brush by or touching. More cleavage is shown or the shorter skirt, the tightest pants or the even tighter shirt to display muscular definition.

Sex is controversy for those who observe it and those who display it. Don't confuse the beauty of the human body with negativity. Anyone can be loved; everyone has a role to play. Sex can be joy if shared. Mutual love can result from the sharing with respect.

However, there are those who use sex as a tool or even a weapon. Why have sex to satisfy your own personal needs, or use sex to control or punish? Some people use sex to enhance one's ego or perceived social status.

Imagine just having sex and discarding partner after partner despite their expressed feelings. To do this is to not allow for attachment, not chancing a relationship. To risk exposing yourself to a relationship, this would require you to commit yourself to a permanent mating partner. This is a risk with a permanent lover. But, this risk could end with rejection and/or failure, the tearful break up. So why risk feelings and just go for the pleasure, the release?

Discarding someone before they get too close or allowing them to fully share themselves with you even though you had no intention of developing anything with them, drama will come as emotional outbursts with anger attached. Phone calls, visits at work or at home are very possible. Notes, cards, flowers or more dramatic measures to get your attention may result.

For most, the act of coupling sexually is the ultimate expression of sharing yourself with someone. These are moments of the mixture of experiences, emotions, energy and responses. Excuse me for being trite here. The cooking of a passionate stew, made with the coming together of two people. This is the ultimate sharing of energy and spirit, the linking of two circles of life.

For some, that expression is beautiful and true. For others, I just described one side of a great 'booty call'. There is so much drama here, this subject demands great caution and care. There is no greater pain than the loss of love or the realization of deception to gain intimacy. Once again, drama in the form of anger and or revenge will follow. It should be noted that the details of your deception will be broadcast, for validation or even sympathy.

Remember, Elementary Thinking says when you add the act of coupling with another; it is very likely to mean that they are sharing their greatest gift with you. If your greed causes you to take and not value this gift, many forms of drama can result without a chance of even starting at just controversy.

Break down the start of a relationship at hello. Be honest; say you're married or sick. Take time if you can. Sometimes there is a chemistry that cannot be ignored, but caution here will never be wrong. Only the best relationships pass the test of time, so build a foundation of time and love using Elemental Thinking.

If you use your sex to manipulate the system, should you not be surprised in failure? If you are using superficial means to succeed, expect the response to your 'self' to be just as superficial. Certainly you should not be offended if you lose your position. You as a person never really got that job, the look of you found success. It was the false look that you used to not allow people to see the real, valuable you. There are plenty of pretty faces, but how much real talent is there in the world?

To sum it up, sex is way too volatile to be handled without a great deal of thought and care. Elementary Thinking can really help here, but using your value set or compassion can work wonders toward your physical and emotional safety. Take your time and lust for the inside, not the outside.

DIAGNOSIS, DRAMA

Without regular doctor visits, drama will sneak up on you when you're not looking. Elementary thinking says be proactive here, not reactive as you pass through your thirties especially. Early detection saves lives, like yours.

Being dead is dramatic, enough said.

The thought that you may regard yourself as ugly or dirty is a bitter pill. These feelings will create a need for renovation of self, often with deadly results. Purging is along the path leading up to this extreme (anorexia) result of self-loathing. This is an example of how you sometimes cannot be enough to your own self. Tattoo art taken to the extreme can be repulsive to others in the workplace or so can too many piercings. Too many plastic surgeries can cause scarring and really give instant recognition to your drama. Do we need to talk about self-mutilation, actually hurting yourself by damaging your gift of life?

Look at yourself in the mirror – are you a doctor? If not, then take your medication as prescribed. Here is another drama machine that is even beyond elementary thinking. Denial often times is a starting symptom when any illness strikes. So when we are prescribed medications to help us by people who have spent six years studying how, why do we not take our doses? "Well, I don't want to because I heard …" Oh really? Are they doctors too?

Hopefully consideration in regard to weight, age and other medications taken are considered. Having all this in place, take your medications. But you feel fine; you don't need to take the full prescription as directed. When you get sick again or the symptoms are prolonged and continuing to prevent your speedy return to work – who is to blame? Not Elementary Thinking. Usually you take antibiotics until they are gone, but you know who you are. When the symptoms subside, you 'save' your antibiotics for next time. Then you wonder why that chest cold became pneumonia. Now, if you take something and you feel worse, contact your physician immediately. Remember Elementary Thinking says there are people who have studied to know more than you … and maybe they really do.

Let's go with the obvious, smoking causes cancer and birth defects when tobacco is used during pregnancy. The drug nicotine is highly addictive and the amount in cigarettes is manipulated by the cigarette companies to make you chemically dependent on them. Your clothes, hair and mouth smell after you smoke. Second hand smoke interacts with non-smokers and especially children adversely. Cigarette smoking can cost anywhere from five to fifty plus dollars weekly. Smoking in bed can kill; restaurants and public buildings do not allow smoking on their premises.

Dramatic? Enough said.

Ever heard of 'crying wolf'? What about the need for attention and asking for 'help'? Often there are too many medical procedures, medications, pain and the numerous calls for medical service. Did you really need the help in sickness or were you just looking for some kindness from a human being?

You took your insulin this morning before you left for work. You showered and dressed, making sure you were ready for your work day. You sat at your desk, doing your work well. All of this care about how you appear to others, but why did you go to the coffee truck and have that breakfast sandwich? You have missed many days due to your sugar imbalance and your doctor says your diabetes will result in the amputation of your right foot. How will you look then?

That was an extreme, but is very common among diabetics. Pass up that extra food filled with carbohydrates and you're all set. Sounds easy? It's not. Elementary Thinking says if I eat this, I can die. But, isn't that worth a few moments of taste pleasure and stomach fullness?

In life, many times our loved ones will be subject to illnesses. Most will be the minor flu-like controversial events we all have shared at one time or another. These events can be problematic, but are for the most part not life altering and or threatening.

When that catastrophic event does strike, Elementary Thinking can play a major role in making even the worst days easier to deal with. Denial will not prepare you for anything; only proactive thinking will get that job done. This is the most important time of all to ask for help, so reach out and put your pride away. This major event in your life is not new in the world, so the majority of resources or experience is free and available. Utilize these resources!

Quietly plan for the worst, it can make a bad situation less overwhelming and give a positive outcome a sweeter taste. Just the simplest acts of preparation can give the greatest relief to a person who does not want to seem like they are a burden. The bonus here is that they can concentrate on self-healing and not be distracted by other things.

Drama here is not participating in the gift of life you have been given. Your loved one is that gift, for all that they are and all that they ever will be to you. Make every effort to share in every aspect of this journey, the good and the bad. This won't be easy sometimes and expect that you may have to make sacrifices. Times may become hard, but your strength will come from the action of your effort. Embrace the small conversations, the handling of medications and physician/hospital visits. Being so involved can lessen the blow of sudden news and can calm the anxiety for yourself and your loved one.

Don't forget that good mental and physical health go hand in hand. If you don't eat well and get enough rest, should you expect to be at your best to heal or help in healing?

In a major illness you can take a proactive approach to really advocate for that friend or loved one. From the very beginning, keep all records and take copious notes about what you are told. Collect any and all reports, results and disks if available. Do not be afraid to ask for records. Bring other family members into the gathering and sharing of information. Use the voice mail message on a single cell phone for a message everyone can listen to. Have a meeting and discuss how and when information will be shared and whom to ask for updates.

Remember, you cannot heal yourself if you are preoccupied with the care you are being given. Elementary Thinkers are the best patient advocates, leaving the patient to concentrate on healing. This advocacy can be medicine for yourself as well as the patient.

Wellness ultimately starts with you. You have only one self, so take care of it. You can't expect to help others if your own health is in question. This questionable health can turn you the rescuer, into the victim.

THE PRICE OF DRAMA

Once upon a time, you could accumulate a huge amount of debt and with a little difficulty, just walk away from your obligation and start all over financially.

THIS IS YOUR WAKE UP CALL!

The party is over. Now, obligations must be met. Not only do you have to repay your creditors, but you will also have that nice bankruptcy on the top of your credit report. In reality, it's better to try to make payment arrangements with your creditors. This is financial drama of the worst kind. Maybe you have seven to ten years of financial life to waste?

Elementary Thinking says back when you opened the credit card, that charge account, borrowed that money, bought that expensive S.U.V., and lived beyond your means. You should have looked ahead to what can result from your actions now, avoid the drama caused by financial tunnel vision.

There are a whole lot of things I could say about overspending, but I think the obvious knowledge of one's limitations kind of sums it all up. Writing checks you really can't cash, both literally and figuratively… Champagne taste, beer pocketbook. You know the rest of the story.

You hear about credit card debt all the time on radio and television. It seems like everyone is sending you a pre-approval for a credit card or store charge card. Welcome to the plastic trap, a hole with trouble at the bottom. Do you realize that if you use more than thirty percent of your available credit on a credit card, you generate a negative credit score if you don't pay it down immediately? Those small available balance cards that take over fifty percent of what they 'give' you in initiation, arrival and monthly fees. Still think all those cards in your wallet are good? By the way, a six dollar monthly fee translates to seventy-two dollars you just give away a year. Can I have it? Just mail it to me since you are feeling so generous.

Others can profit from your drama and they have no problem doing it.

Can you create wealth by making better choices? If you had a choice between a condominium and a home of your own, which would you choose? If you value privacy, a condominium with its close quarters is not for you. If you like to have complete control over your parking, having a driveway at a home of your own is perfect.

So, we know about the little human things, but what about costs? In most condos you own the inside, but not the outside. Someone has to pay for the mowing of the grass, the shoveling and plowing of the snow. Oh yes, that 'condo' fee.

A single mother has three children to feed on a monthly assistance allowance. However, at the grocery store, she makes numerous bad food choices. Too many snacks and luxury foods to impress a boyfriend are purchased. Fast forward to the end of the month, no bread or milk in the kitchen and no new allowance until the first of the month.

Drama? You bet!

Now she must look for alternate sources to make up for the nutritional shortfall. This out of mind and body fantasy is not only poisoning to herself, but often there are children or other family members present.

What about that shoe fetish? You know that pair of open toe beauties cost way too much, but why not skip the electric bill this month?

The 'girls' at the office will be so impressed. Don't pay your bills and watch the drama fire burn out of control. While you are playing catch up, you wind up making smaller payments on other bills. As this starts to spin out of control, other bills are neglected or underpaid. But those shoes sure do make you look hot!

The stock market can often become a good source of revenue with a little 'help' from your broker. Funny thing though, the broker arrives in a Mercedes and wears a tailored suit. Did you cash that big dividend check lately? A healthy stock portfolio can reap great benefits with a well-developed and read prospectus along with good financial planning at home. By the way, did you recognize all of the fees associated with the transactions associated with your trading account? Some of these fees may seem small, but their accumulation can offset or even surpass dividends. How does this make sense?

Putting your head in the sand is never a solution obviously, so a proactive move needs to be made in order to arrest any further problems before they develop. The solution begins with the realization that things are out of control and need to be fixed, NOW!

Feeling better by wearing designer clothes, or leasing that expensive car, is not the answer. I heard a joke the other day ... "You know you're 'ghetto' if your rims are worth more than your car".

Unless you are Bill Gates, I figure you are not rich enough. So, shouldn't we think before spending?

So now that we have determined that we are poor, what are our alternatives? Saving for a 'rainy day' is what Elementary Thinking is all about. A good bet is always to save, but why not sure? Saving at home has a theft risk associated with it, so the bank probably will work best.

Making better choices is what this book is all about. Think about coupon cutting and comparison shopping by reading labels and product descriptions. Don't fall into the convenience traps set for you. Companies know that you like things at your fingertips or quick to use. So, they will charge you more to save time. But, what's the real savings in time versus money?

Imagine a world where you take several minutes on the evening before and made lunch for yourself. Imagine it with healthy choices and the money you would save. What? Using my own, clean, healthy choices for lunch? Not having to spend money for lunch is a savings, right?

Making choices in energy use are as important as any clothing or make-up choice. Remove incandescent bulbs, lower the thermostat at home. You can use weather-stripping and energy saving appliances in your effort. Small choices to add up to a big savings, money saved to fight drama.

Remember, if something looks too good to be true, it usually is. Rushing to make choices is not being pro-active with every day mistakes, it's just plain stupid. A real good example of this is the mortgage sub-prime lending crisis of 2007. No money down, bad credit or no credit. Sounded like a great way to get into that first home or a better one, right? But, what about that adjustable interest rate? Because you're a sub-prime borrower your rate is high and the monthly payments you make are pretty high. The markets change and the `rate adjustment' takes your high payments and sends them to a point that even the best borrower is left without means to make the monthly payments. Default and foreclosure are the usual dramatic result, ending your homeownership dream. Research and read the fine print before moving forward. Wait to put yourself in a more vested position before going into a mortgage is the Elemental Thinkers view.

At the beginning of this chapter I spoke about financial tunnel vision leading to big drama. But, armed with Elementary Thinking you can naturally minimize damage and pro-act limiting the negative results of bad choices before they become dramatic.

DRAMATIC DIVISION

Pardon me for stating the obvious, but no two human beings are alike. This is where the drama begins and it is as diverse as we are as humans. I will touch on a few issues of division; add your own if needed. I'm sure I will think of more once this book is published, but here goes.

Racial division is a favorite topic of mine, and not because of its negative nature. It will always bring about conversation and I'm amazed how this subject can turn a person's intellect off like a switch. Racial issues are often as strong as the negative stereotypes associated with them. Fear and intolerance go hand in hand as a shield against common sense and a truly common thread, the human element.

Here's where I get myself into trouble. I don't understand where the descriptive nature of the assignment of colors to races comes from. For example, brown skinned people are referred to as black if they originate from Africa. Black always reminded me as the remnant from fire which had consumed, and left charcoal and or ashes.

Black Holes are observed in space as pulling in everything around them into their eternal abyss. So, they suck, absorb and give nothing back. Black is scary, the shadows, the dark, it's what we fear after death.

If you are descended from Africa, you're black. But, if you have brown skin from other places you're not black. What if you are a descendant from southern Italy, or Sicily? Brown skinned, but not black.

South America? You're South American or Bolivian, whatever. Cuba, you're Hispanic or Cuban. Mongolia, Mongolian or Chinese.

If you are from Asia, you are considered yellow. But, if you are from China, you can be red or yellow. "The robber, a black man, was taken into custody." All of these colors, who decides who gets what color and what is a good or bad color?

I guess we have to further qualify what we are afraid of or don't understand. Fear and ignorance create and widen the gaps between people. We teach this drama to our children so they can spread our gospel of hatred and intolerance. What they see is what they do.

Religions teach separation, which seems ugly and hurtful to me. You can't marry outside of your faith in a lot of cases. If you continue to worship, why should you be damned for love? Intolerance is often gospel here, taught as other faiths are inferior. Only you and your faith will be redeemed, reach enlightenment, sit at the table in Valhalla, be at the feet of Allah, and ascend to heaven with Christ. There are many more examples of the cleansing of the spirit and it's preparation for an afterlife.

Please believe that I have a spiritual faith, but under no circumstances do I advocate fear through intolerance of other faiths. These dramatic divisions have kept our planet on a par boil for thousands of years. There have been so many crusades and wars, inquisitions, public executions and torture. All of this to humiliate, to inspire conversion with human interpretation of the gospel.

Read any of the 'good books' and then read my chapter on Elemental Thinking. No preaching here, just positive energy and no intolerance. A message that any religion or person cannot belong, means the rest of the world is hopelessly doomed. Lucky for you to stumble upon the perfect word given to us. But, why the wars and killing on behalf of the faith?

Social divisions begin very early in life. We learn to find comfort in 'people like us'. Forming small groups to fit in or belong as we start to learn how to be people. As we grow older, the real divisions become very apparent in preparation for young adulthood. This is provided that you don't go to a boarding school for high school. This will separate you even more from the mainstream. Either way, normal or boarding, high school begins the great divide. Do you study, play sports, cheer lead, farm, govern, get high or just gossip?

Early social divisions will set the course for your life. Ultimately, persons who are not proactive will find drama and it won't be the first time. As you grow old going to the same bar, having the same friends and the same dreams of what could have been as you order yet another drink. That dream is drama, not choosing another path and being too old to go back to school or even care. Would have, could have, and should have. Way too much drama, I guess you just are who you are now.

Someone walks into your life that hasn't seen you in about forever. But, you've changed your mindset, values, spiritual focus and think proactive. Here they come and you're on the new and better path. Will they ever know when you made better choices? They only see the result of now. Is this the time machine you were looking for?

In our society, the economic divisions between average persons are canyons or oceans apart. Once upon a time in America, we had a stepped system of economic position. You were poor, middle class, affluent or very rich. Now we have the homeless and poor, affluent or super rich. The middle class are gone, dropping into the poor paycheck to paycheck pot. The homeless and poor are together because homelessness is so rampant and many of the poor live in such areas of disrepair, vermin and insect infestation. Conditions so poor, that they are living in a non-home.

The dramatic divide between the classes, rich and poor, leaves little room for growth that you can see economically. However, Elemental Thinkers are we. Drama does not like us, because maintaining purity of thought and with your circle of life; you can bridge the economic division. It's slow going, but small slow steps are always the safest. Watch a baby trying to walk and they don't know anything about drama yet. Stepping and just testing slowly, until the positive end result.

Ethnicity and national pride are to be cherished. If an immigrant or descended from one, it's remembrances of home.

It's a journey and start in a new land made with courage and a spirit of adventure. However, don't confuse pride in the home of your ancestors, with your home now. If a citizen, remember that you are an

American. Don't forget your roots, but don't place yourself in a position where your patriotism is questioned. Get a good feel for this, use Elemental Thinking. Don't be like some who only display the flag of their ancestor's country, on their clothing and vehicles. This is in your face dramatic and is the wrong mindset for joining and being a part of the melting pot which is America. Don't be afraid to be proud to be an American. Display the 'stars and stripes' on your car or home, the power of the American spirit is drama repellent.

In a capitalist society like ours, it's all about acquiring more capital, more market share, the bigger house, the luxury car, the sexiest mate, the best job. And of course, MORE MONEY! As you grab more and more, you obviously set you and yours apart from the rest of us sheep. When your division is setting yourself apart with wealth, a whole long list of dramatic descriptors come to mind. Envy, theft, vandalism, taxes, registration, misuse, bad feelings among siblings, etc. Make your American dreams come true, but remember all eyes will be on you. Those eyes will not be looking for opportunities to praise you.

Some things are such a natural irritant in conversation as adults. The greatest catalyst for argument is making comments about our political leaders. A natural division is built in, the two party system. This system requires a choice between two schools of thought, the liberal Democratic mule stubborn tack or the Republican conservative elephant large think tank. Let's not forget the Independent voting block under many different names, Communist, Green, Peoples, Independent or whatever you can use for a name and add party after it.

Any or all of these groups are asking for and expect a voice in our political system at election time. The two main parties have the power and monies to control the mainstream of political thought. The Independents are often self-financed and closer to the 'big two'.

Republicans and Democrats trade control over government regularly, one side controlling for a few years and nothing gets done. Then, the other side gains control on this feeling of nothing done, and then they do the same thing. We vote them out and replace them with the other. Meanwhile, we ignore all of the other candidates because they don't have the money, reputation or message to be in the mainstream. And of course, they are unknown, so they can't be normal like us.

Independents are just that, independent of the normal thought of the 'big two'. Support here means that you are not part of the mainstream and are liberal beyond the point of no return. I think this makes you clearly divided from the divided 'big two' and from the little political fish.

Once elected, there is a majority and a minority and their leaders vie for control of votes to make laws. They are divided inside and out, so are they with us? Lobbyists can create even more division by wooing politicians with gifts and monetary considerations. Considerations? What about giving our political leaders cash or favors to vote for ideas. That divides them from us and is often dramatically illegal or at the very least dramatically unethical.

I'm a huge fan of Dr. Stephen Hawking, an Einsteinesque thinker in the age we live in. Not only is this man huge in thought, but he should be huge in the fact that he is in a wheelchair and has limited use of his body. Yet his mind is one of the greatest to ever give to our civilization words of wisdom, words he can only speak with a computer voice. So you look at the man in the wheelchair, he's not like us. He doesn't look smart, does smart have a look? The greatest minds on our planet wait for his next words, his vision. Yet, he is not like them, more beautiful in thought than they will ever be his being mute only a gift.

So, what's the division here? People with medical conditions or deformities are just like us, they are us. I remember a woman I had met as a first responder; she was having a diabetic incident. She was unable to move and apparently very conscious as I later found out. She said she saw everything I did and heard everything I said. She said she felt trapped in her body, unable to respond, unable to make me understand what she was feeling.

The division is people and we should not judge them for not being normal. Even though we have made normal a societal perception, all people need a voice across division. Their reality is waking up each and every day as themselves, their version of normal. We, divided from their world, are the strange intolerant ones.

What do you get if you mix ethnic, geographic and cultural differences? Ethnic cleansing, genocide, mass imprisonment, mass rape and other types of violence and or intolerance in the name of diversity. The burning of books, religious persecution, closing of borders help to keep the divide between your thoughts and mine.

Recently, I sat and thought about my own difficulties with racial diversity and intolerance and something struck me. I know this is going to get me in all kinds of trouble, but here goes.

In the United States, the largest minority population is now Hispanic or Spanish speaking. Seeing this, I offer the following observations for dramatic discussion. Let's start with information provided in English and Spanish. Now, if you were interested in empowering a people, would you enable them to continue to be divided from mainstream America? I'm not talking about helping; I'm talking about children born in the United States having to be taught English. The printing of English and Spanish on government forms, groceries and bills only keeps the divide intact. You can't self-empower here, it's a system made to enable division.

Money is printed in English, do stockbrokers and bankers speak Spanish? Spanish is predominately spoken in the inner-city or in poorer communities. The chains of intolerance or diversity do not have to be wrapped around our ankles to be felt. With black people, it was segregation from basic services right down to public toilets and 'whites only' water fountains. It extended to schools, colleges and the right to vote.

This division will continue to prevent our Hispanic population from joining the way of life all Americans are entitled to. Using language to block self-empowerment is a truly insidious and covert tactic to create and promote division, not diversity.

I know I wrote an awful lot of stuff and you may agree or disagree with some of it. But, guess what? If you or someone you know is talking about the examples I just gave you about division, then the author did his job. The only real way to bridge any divide is to start with a line of communication. Once that line crosses the great divide, now you have something to build from and on, good or bad.

In many of my examples, self-empowerment is ongoing and gains can be seen daily. Others will pass the test of time, the ignorance and intolerance fed to the next generation.

This author believes in diversity not division, open dialog, not closed door intolerance. In high school, I was voted most argumentative in my senior class. I guess as a young man, I would rather agree to disagree.

Not much has changed.

DRAMA PHOBIA

Triskaidekaphobia is a fear of the number 13. It is usually considered to be a superstition. A specific fear of Friday the 13th is called triskaidekaphobia.

Thirteen may be considered a "bad" number, simply because it is one more than twelve. Twelve is a popularly used number in many cultures (due to it being a highly composite number). When a group of 13 objects is divided into two, three, four, or six equal groups, there is always one leftover object.

The number 13 also retains biblical meanings. At the Last Supper, Judas, the disciple who betrayed Jesus, was the 13th to sit at the table (also spilling the salt).

It has also been linked to the fact that a luni-solar calendar must have 13 months in some years, while the solar Gregorian calendar and lunar Islamic calendar always have 12 months in a year.

Triskaidekaphobia may have also affected the Vikings - it is believed that Loki in the Norse pantheon was the 13th god. This was later Christianized into saying that Satan was the 13th angel.

Some buildings number their floors so as to skip the thirteenth floor entirely, jumping from floor 12 to floor 14 in order to avoid distressing triskaidekaphobics, or using 12 and 12b instead. One Canada Square in Canary Wharf, the tallest building in the UK, lacks a 13th floor. Most hotel/casino mega-resorts in Las Vegas also lack a 13th floor. This is sometimes applied to house or room numbers as well. The same is also true of rows in airplanes.

In the Disney film 'The Rescuers', one of the main characters; the mouse Bernard is highly triskaidekaphobic, refusing to step on the thirteenth step of a ladder or stairway. He is shocked to discover however, that his flight on Orville the albatross is Flight Thirteen.

American singer-songwriter John Mayer had 14 tracks on his album 'Room for Squares' although the 13th is 0.2 seconds of silence and is not listed on the album cover. Likewise, Hot Heat's album 'Elevator' does not list a 13th track on its cover. On the CD the 13th track is four seconds of random noise.

Some refer to the near-fatal Apollo 13 mission to the moon as proof of 13 being unlucky. Apollo 13 was launched at 14:13 EST on April 11, 1970 (4/11/70, digits summing up to 13) from complex 39 (three times thirteen). Widespread rumors that it launched at 13:13 local time (EST) are incorrect, although it is true that this correspond to 13:13 CST the local time in Houston, Texas, the location of mission control. Apparently, Apollo 13 was also going to go through LOI Lunar Orbit Injection on April 13th. Others have noted that while that for a supposedly unlucky mission, the fact that the crippling accident occurred when the crew was best equipped to cope with it, is a lucky occurrence in itself.

The Spanish motor racer Angel Nieto is famous for saying that he achieved *12 + 1* World Motorcycling Championships. A bio-pic about him is thus titled 12 + 1.

The characters Stan and Hilda Ogden, in the English TV series Coronation Street, lived at 12a Coronation Street to avoid their address being number 13.

In Formula 1, there is no car with the number 13. The number has been removed after 2 drivers were killed in crashes - both driving cars numbered 13; however cars without the number 13 regularly crash as well.

The arrest and murder of the Knights Templar occurred on Friday, 13th October 1307.

Memphis International Airport in Memphis, TN does not have a Gate A13, B13, or C13. Also, the Birmingham International Airport in Alabama does not contain a Gate C13.

I guess in a pure departure for Elementary Thinking, just cross your fingers and hope for luck.

DRAMA BY MISDIRECTION

Often, persons will try to limit their drama at your expense. Remember when you got into trouble as a child? You were told that you did it and you got caught. But didn't the other kid do it too? Be wary of people who tell you that they are o.k. when they are really just as messed up as the rest of the world.

We all have problems, but there is an element out there that cannot deal with their own reality, so they will deflect attention away from themselves in order to lessen or limit the responsibility for their own actions.

For example, a person may be embroiled in a controversy of their own making in the workplace. Instead of taking responsibility for their own actions, they will create a diversion by perhaps telling a supervisor that another employee was late. Even divulging secrets shared in confidence about a fellow employee is not out of bounds. You may have a family member in a time of crisis speak of their own problems to show that they are in need of the focus of the family's attention. They may even go so far as to become silent to illicit the "are you okay?"

Why would a major movie actress shoplift? Is there a psychiatric pathology at work? Chemical dependence? I am sure that she does not want the negative publicity. But, is she really diverting away from her fears, low self-esteem, and the need for medical intervention?

Recognition of one's weaknesses as controversial potential is the key to self-help and diminished drama.

How many times have you heard about a fire and a body was found when the fire was put out? Then you heard it was really a homicide. That's probably the most vivid example of misdirection, but it still applies. Drama to cover drama, making the worst out of an already bad situation.

Initially, you may not spot the misdirection, but gathering early information about your surroundings, including the people in it can't hurt. Don't walk into situations blindly; tunnel vision can block your ability to see trouble ahead.

The realization of failure or defeat can be more than just painful. It can be so profound to self, almost like being in shock. When this happens, the first thing you want to do is go primal ... Flight or fight.

Misdirectors are the perfect example of the flight instinct. They do not want to be themselves, so they want to run away ... But how? You can't leave your body and you can't stop being who you are. Taking the focus off anything negative is like an inner cloaking device. This is a shield from the hills and valleys of life, right?

Alert! Misdirectors truly believe in their self causes and will sacrifice anything but themselves.

Remember to assess the elements of controversy when initially dealing with others. You may save yourself some drama of your own by breaking down a person's actions or psyche into smaller, more easily digestible pieces.

Sometimes ask yourself why, when a person speaks.

By placing yourself in situations that are more wholesome and realizing when situations are not, can shield you from a great deal of drama tossed in your direction.

Take responsibility for your own life and spend time on keeping your daily path in focus. Focus on what's at your feet as well as what's on the horizon.

Can you surrender? It doesn't take low self-esteem, it takes real guts. You have to decide that you have had enough and that you truly want to win, to achieve and soar above the drama. Drama is the dirty water in the tub of your life. At some point, you decide that you are clean for now and ready to face the world. As you watch the water circle and swirl around and down the drain, don't you ever wish that your life could be cleansed in the same way?

When you surrender, you stop and assess where you are now. Don't look back, look forward. Make believe that there is no past you, that was then. If your reset is true, the future will fall into place like the pieces of a puzzle.

This is the responsibility that you must and only you can assume. Stand and say, "I did this and only I can fix it." After you say it, write it down and look at it.

Write down a goal for the day that you can reach with a plan. It's the plan that you write down, with a goal in mind.

Now that you can see it, you have something that you can achieve today.

"I want to tell twenty of my loved ones today that I love them."

"I want to tell ten of my co-workers that I appreciate something that they did for me."

Can you do something that easy? Try it, first.

Thank the letter carrier today or promise that you will spend fifteen minutes with each of the kids today and ask them about school and their day.

Stop your drama cold by setting goals you can reach and make yourself stronger. Pushing or directing negative energy around only spreads negative energy around.

I gave you some ideas on how to self-empower. But, the greatest way to find strength is not by being closed off to the world. The greatest strength is to realize that you need help and are willing to surrender and ask another for it. A mistake does not have to be a negative event.

Steer yourself away from drama by directing your energy toward something good, direct your energy down a path others can follow.

If you get caught up in misdirecting yourself, I guess you need to ask yourself why. Think of this, when you are hurt physically, a period of healing must take place. The healing is a repair, eventual lessening of pain and a return to function.

Drama is an injury to your life that needs your immediate intervention. But, when you allow drama to accumulate and catch up to you, don't misdirect, direct and repair.

This intervention is the beginning of self-empowerment, you rebuilding you. Using Elementary Thinking, you will see what is wrong. But, will you be able to heal? Healing begins with the now and stabilizing the wobble in your circle of life. But, a full assessment of your injury includes what caused the problem in the first place.

Often the worst part of an injury is the scar tissue that is left. A re-injury of this area will require twice as long to heal. So, that drama that keeps coming back around will only require more time and effort to repair and will add layers or scarring. What is scarring anyway?

Failed relationships provide the deepest injuries and scars. Scars are really time-released drama, a product of our lack of prompt intervention.

If you're scarred deeply, do you deal with problems or live in denial. Can you help others, raise children or otherwise be able to maintain relationships if your perception is clouded when dealing with your own drama?

Forgiveness is the start of your return to non-dramatic health. Don't be so hard on yourself that you become blinded to that dramatic anchor you drag behind you. Life is hard enough, but how can you use Elementary Thinking with so much in the back of your mind?

Forgive yourself, you are only human. Perfection is a goal, but not a reality. So that past of yours, needs to be embraced. Misdirection can be saying goodbye to someone, but never really dealing with the separation. This can be both in life and in death.

Forgive others, they are only human. Their perfection is an expectation of yours, but not a reality. This is a hard thing to do, but you will feel 'clean' afterwards. In addition, you will add to your self-empowerment and enhance your ability to be more open and accepting in relationships.

Imagine that lover you lost, someone who hurt you. Hurt, dramatic injury? Makes you act differently than you normally would to be safe, right? If you are changing the way you respond to someone because of an injury, you are misdirecting yourself away for protection.

I'm not talking about physical abuse, which I do not condone. This is about when relationships end and emptiness remains, a scar. Lovers, siblings, comrades or acquaintances and all can be gone away with a lasting effect. This effect varies from outward and overt, to trapped within your soul and deep into your core.

In this example, the bond you lost needs closure. Until the door is closed in your mind, drama will result. Keeping it simple, it's an itch you need to scratch, but can't. Can you take charge and self-empower? Elemental Thinking can shrink this drama into small bite sized pieces of controversy.

How? What about making a gesture toward this dramatic injury? Make a phone call and say thank you for the good moments you had and goodbye or least leave 'the door' open on your own terms, with good words and not anger.

If the person reacted badly and you were wrong, you tried to offer words of responsibility. You surrendered your pride and it was in vain. But, now you can move on knowing it wasn't meant to be. In your mind, you should now realize that you made the final effort. You were the bigger one and have the power.

Use forgiveness and early intervention to self-empower. By setting daily goals and surrendering to the realization that you are not perfect. By taking responsibility for what you do and for what you have done, you can take charge of what left you with scars and truly heal. No more misdirecting, taking on anyone and anything.

THE DRAMA OF LOVE

What is warm and consuming? What is carefree and makes the pulse pound? What will make the skin tingle and perspiration fall like rain? What will put arsenic in tea and pass a lie over the lips? What can bond for life or a reckless day?

Initially, I tried to avoid the subject. But, if you really want to talk about drama, how could you possibly avoid the subject of love and its power. The power to bring such joy and to inflict pain described as or in the name of love.

Love is often associated with the heart, supposedly being within or symbolized by. Love is not a muscle - it's a feeling and a state of being. It's a way of life and a conscious choice of offering self to another. It's an invisible bond that can be represented in so many ways. This representation can make the bond even stronger.

We love our parents and siblings, bonded to them by home life and D.N.A. Some of our friends we love bonded to them by shared experiences. Even though the love represented here is mostly non-physical, these are the strongest types of love and the most spiritual. These bonds are the true family bonds and even blood will be shed in their defense.

In your immediate circle of friends and family, the drama will run strong. You know who these people are and at the holidays, they come out to play. I don't want to diminish the drama generated throughout the year, but let's talk about real trouble. When you mix family or friends and alcohol, you get big drama. How big? Because of being a family member or close friend, I guess you just relax a little more than usual. Emotions, alcohol and a high comfort level ... Drama!

Comedian Bill Cosby once said in a monologue, "people take drugs because it enhances their personality ..." His punch line was, "well what if you're an ***hole?"

Alcohol is a drug.

So at the family Christmas party, there's food and alcohol. Often, there is more alcohol than food. It's amazing how these situations can cause even the most forgetful person to have perfect memory. Ah yes, the most embarrassing moments in your life are now available for re-view. This is a serious test of Elementary Thinking and you cannot even be close to being 'thin-skinned' here.

Remembrances of things you did while young and immature. No subject is taboo and once it starts, everyone has their favorite story at your expense. If you brought a friend, date or new spouse to the gather-ing, the drama is the damage control you may have to do later. Getting caught up in the joke and trying to show everyone that they're funny can leave you socially naked.

Resist the urge to burn 'bridges' here. By biting your tongue, you will save numerous other family relationships. You should be able to rely upon the family bond to protect you. This bond should give you comfort in even your darkest moments.

Want more drama explanation?

Some of your greatest enemies can often be your own family mem-bers. You need to be careful to avoid them and remember not to offend as you go. This balancing act is the hardest thing you will ever have to do in your life. Family or enemy? How can someone so close to you, want to stab you so deeply?

Often while you use Elemental Thinking, some in the world around you are oblivious to common sense. So, don't have an expecta-tion that with family you can find refuge. Each member will earn and display their 'stripes' to you, keep your eyes and mind open.

This is not an indictment of family relationships and love. If you are mature enough to read this, you already have had an ample sampling of the immediate and extended family. So, use caution before judgment here. A small amount of negative energy projected here will be returned multiplied many times.

This is a book about drama and this is the love chapter, so I guess I should talk about love versus trust and family. I've spent a lot of time in the family drama, because we can all relate. With family, we are born into an instant relationship with a degree of natural love and trust built in. Here comes some big drama, deep stuff.

As we enter this world, our lives are an empty slate. We are ready to absorb information to build the foundation of who we are. Love here is the bond between ourselves and those who gave us life. The love here is also our bond with those we share an origin with...siblings. As human beings, we equate love with trust and trust with love. Love and trust being the expression of this bond.

As adults, we already have defense mechanisms in place, love and trust filters for our protection. So when young, we trust our parents to make choices for us to survive and to nurture us. Based upon limited experience, we expect older or persons in authority to look out for our best interest. In some extreme cases, drama comes in the form of abusing this trust. This abuse will be described as love, it really is only synonymous with self-benefit.

The abuse of trust I speak of can be the start of sibling rivalry, telling a fib or breaking a toy. It could also be inappropriate touching or other sexual relationship described as love from an older sibling, family member or other person. Remember that love and trust are precious gifts. Inexperience is not a fault, it's a clean view. It's a perfectly clear view, untouched by negative perception.

The real drama here is the realization that someone used without value, your precious and shiny gift of love and trust. Too often this vision comes well after you have dusted yourself off, swept the dirt away into some dark corner. Dirt is still dirt, swept over here or over there. Dirt is only a metaphor here, your gift was shiny and clean, you didn't tarnish it.

As you grow older and wiser, you remember your gift. Is it really tarnished or do you still have it? I guess you have to ask yourself if you made a conscious choice to do something, right or wrong. If you didn't make a choice, then believe that you are still really clean, shiny and bright. Even in repetition, you did not make the initial choice and never had enough information to choose. Love? This was an advantage taken, a theft of innocence that you could not prevent.

Elementary Thinking says, forgive yourself and let go of the old anger. It is anger that you have carried around forever. Which, believe it or not, is just helping to keep a negative past alive. By the way, if your vessel for love is now filled with this that you did not create, how can you truly heal? How can you return to that shiny and new clean you? Love must always begin with you, love yourself and live. It's a really basic and simple method; the start of the healing does not have to be complicated. It only needs to be started by a person ready to surrender, ready to realize that you are a good person and full of love.

Any discussion about love needs to have mention about symbolism in its regard. First, there are so many acts that can be real expressions of love and also generic and bland without feeling. Drama is the projection or the reception of this 'love'. Its real meaning when used is the blueprint for your journey through life. Relationships will come and go throughout most lives, why try and risk failure? It's the great chance at success, based upon our needs. What does need have to do with love? Need is nothing more than desire plus expectation. Or, is need a crank to insert into love to make passion?

Ah, yes, the 'L' word. Love is the gateway toward your ability to gain favor in a relationship or maybe just a coupling advantage. Love is still a powerful and good thing even though I have to give examples of pain and sometimes suffering. Hang in there, love can be beautiful.

I spoke earlier about the love and trust bonds formed as we enter this world. Believe me, I'm sure all of our parents meant well and had good intentions. However, for some, the expectation that they will parent well is outside of the curve.

Parenting is instinctual, a roll of the dice or a shot in the dark. There are many guides, books, courses or other forms of learning out there. But, it's really up to each and every one of us to make the right choices on our own. I guess we try look to each other to accomplish this huge task. Surely, a great deal of trial and error paves the way. So when does parental love stop nurturing? Also, when should the making of parental choices for our children stop?

I guess we should start with the dramatic basics. As young ladies trying to find an identity, some changes must be made in order to be able to move forward into young adulthood. Maybe a little make-up or dressing with a little more 'appeal'. As this passage takes place, moms and dads everywhere rebel, demanding that makeup and those clothes be removed and or changed. Is your obeying love or just yielding to their authority? Parents, is this love or are you not allowing your daughter to grow up, beyond your control?

Drama here comes in the forms of rebellion displayed, just like sneaking out of the house before getting caught. Numerous arguments with parents and refusals to cooperate are a part of this. A level of tension now develops, is love still here? Of course it is, but cooperation is the key and that is love too. Drama also is that need to produce carbon copies of ourselves, our enduring legacy. Ever hear of the word smothering?

The lack of parenting can be just as dramatic. Development without guidance or example can allow for a bad start to life through experimental mistakes. Experimental mistakes are made as you try to develop as a person, while others are trying to influence you. Often, you can easily get caught up in other people's bad choices. Love is being there to help out as a parent with young choices. The love is the helping and the giving. The real trick is the balance between parental control and the emergence of a new person.

Drama is also here in the form of trying to live a new life through your children. It's hard to have lived your life and lost, but give your kids a break. This is a really good time to work on Elementary Thinking as a tool for young survival. Parental obsession is drama, spending so much time trying to keep control of someone. When the children leave the 'nest', it is truly a leap of faith.

There is a certain element of respect that is tempered with love. It really shows just how much love and family are intertwined, especially between parents and children.

Family love drama can be as simple as a few of the wrong words or adding that one extra drink. This only scratches the surface and I'm just getting started.

Using your family bond to borrow or obtain favor is not the way to go. When you allow these sins, the results are far reaching and terrible. Think about a small cash loan that doesn't get repaid. How do you collect and not risk alienating certain factions of your extended family. It's funny how you gave a loan in love as family. But now, you are just another evil lender, just trying to collect a debt and you deserve to be repaid. By the way, of course these loans are interest free. Hey, it is family that you're lending to.

Love in action, a way of doing things. The action of love, this through doing things for your loved ones. Selfless acts in the name of and for family, based upon the bonds families have and or love. Do I sound cynical if I say that, for some, family means implied consent to take advantage?

Relationships have a tendency to create drama, asked for or not. This is another one of those touchy subjects and I'm already in the deep pool on this one, so let's swim around.

I once heard from a friend that she really hurt a guy that she was seeing. She also told me that she had little regard for men in relationships and felt that she should hurt or use them. Her policy was them before me. The guy had told her that he loved her and demonstrated it in positive ways.

That should draw drama like a magnet by starting with the negative relationship mindset, then a break up event. But, here is the rest of the story. He showered her with gifts and pleas to return to their relationship. After a period of seeing this she gave in, they went out to dinner and nature took its course. They went back to her apartment and made love, or so she thought. They had sex, the man was rough and when he finished, he put his clothes on. He then left her there, not saying a word and they never spoke again.

Drama here is when you invest so much of yourself in someone; you have expectations and hopes of reaping the rewards of your open and loving effort. If you don't respect this loving gift, should you expect loving back in return? Remember; don't expect Elementary Thinking to protect your lack of good choices. Common sense and class are not inherited and can't be acquired, only learned.

Love is like a shoehorn, getting into the tightest of mind sets. It is the result of one of life's most abstract things, the balance of simple emotion. For something that is not tangible, much violence has consumed the soul of civilization in the name of emotion and in acts of love.

Love has a special component, its real basis. We do not know where it comes from, but we can make it even stronger. It's that cyclic thing here I talk about so often. Become emotional, love results. Be in love and your emotions add cement to the loving mix. As the love grows deeper, so does the emotional response and so on.

Love, it is said is blind. This is why I talk about Elementary Thinking as a lifestyle, a lifestyle that will instinctively take over even in the event of blinding emotion.

In this book as in life, one of the most potent forms of personal expression is the acts surrounding intimacy. I spoke about this in an earlier chapter, but its relevance here can't be overlooked. Intimacy is often given as a gift of open passage or sharing based upon emotions or what is perceived as love. These acts are also an expression of a bond or want to be bonded.

Drama here is intercourse, the ultimate expression of bonding, the act of sex. Let's not forget, these acts can be between heterosexual, bisexual or homosexual persons. Fellatio, cunnilingus, actual intercourse or other stimulation will set the drama cycle in motion.

If you begin the bonding process and are hoping for an opportunity at intimacy, 'Elementary Thinking' says use caution. Ever heard of 'the one night stand'? I know you have, so why be surprised when the storm comes. Emotional radar exists in each and every one of us. Who wants to get their feelings hurt on purpose?

Earlier in this chapter, I spoke about the woman who gave of her intimacy freely and accepted the intimate response coupled with emotion given to her. She accepted his gift of emotion and allowed for the acts of bonding. The dates, gifts, sleeping together and otherwise acting like a couple, all that bonding is.

She was hurt and otherwise offended when her before lover took his pleasure as a statement about or an expression of his anger. So, why should she be upset? One sided thinking or being selfish blocked the real feeling which should have guided her in intimacy. He took revenge, using the act of love as a weapon.

They both lost.

In the previous example, was it love, emotions or desire that created the drama? Desire says 'I think you look yummy, you're a ` hottie.' So, you go with the simple physical attraction, the simple it looks good. If you set the rules when you start, o.k. waste intimacy, steal some pleasure and roll the dice.

Let's sum up and move on. Intimacy, a.k.a. intercourse, should be handled with care. Don't just assume feelings won't play a part in decision making here, either yours or theirs. The more often engaged with the same partner, the more likelihood that drama will result.

Drama has a way of creeping even into what seems like the most simplistic of situations. Do you think animals can emotionally bond with humans? Animals can develop learned behavior, so why not adjust how they act based upon the tone of your voice or even their perception of your mood.

I made a funny and striking observation about a frequent traveler and her feline companion. The kitty was well behaved for the most part, with daily interaction on its own terms of course. Until...the suitcases came out. Now kitty becomes a Tasmanian Devil, running around the house smelling the luggage and begging for attention. Is this an emotional response or even love? Is the feline basing its display on the smells associated with the departure of its master? Never noticed? Now you will. Don't think that such sophisticated creatures cannot have emotions or even feel love towards you. You touch them literally and the caresses we take for granted are acts of intimacy to them. They take pleasure in this interaction, bonding with us the true focal point in their lives.

The drama here is the lack of perception that we have to the amount of stimulus we generate and our relationship with the creatures we take into our homes. So when the animals 'mark' or scratch on valuable carpets, furniture, or that special item gets chewed and otherwise damaged, who is really to blame?

Animals can possess Elementary Thinking as learned behavior for the most part, so what's your excuse? Others, including your pet friends, can develop relationships with you. This is the bonding that you could transcend into emotion or love. Use this gift wisely and with your eyes open. Don't squander it's pure and special value.

Speaking of love, ever pour what seemed like everything into what you thought was a relationship? And then, all of a sudden it's over. It sure was something you couldn't walk away from easily, so how could your partner? Why couldn't they see how valuable you are? So full of love you are, giving gifts and making dinner. All those phone calls, flowers, time at your place. Didn't those things mean anything? Why did the dialog stop? They wanted the intimacy, that precious gift that you had to give. But in the end, they still walked away.

The obvious drama here is your being left feeling empty and feeling like you were used to enhance someone for a brief period of time. You are left with a feeling that this relationship should be saved. Saved? So your pride should be abandoned? You want to recover what you lost and no cost is too great, right? Drama here is the person who has no idea who you really are and doesn't care. So, off you go on your quest and the chase is on. Pitching but no one is catching. This kind of drama is so ugly; it's one-sided and very dangerous.

Of course there is never a remembrance of the damage done overall, the big cyclic picture getting lost in emotion. It really takes a big picture view without blinders on to get over this loss. This is a view that needs to be taken by both parties in this dramatic play.

Love has many options in its creation. Could it be said that some of us actually go looking for love, as if it has a place where we can find it. Remember, love is abstract and tough to even hold on to. Trying to find or recover love is like trying to predict what tomorrow will bring. When you go on a search, human nature and fatigue will cause you to settle. To settle is when you overlook what you need for what you want right now. It is rushing into bringing another untested personality into your life.

Drama is, as you settle you overlook that nasty comment or habit. Maybe even an odor you just don't like or selfishness in bed. Those are a few quick ones, but not too much farther down the road comes the real drama. A perfect union is a by-product of the bonding process and that takes time. As time passes, things start to emerge about that other person that you never took the time to find out. Do you think it's dramatic to end a relationship with a person who thought they were evaluated and found to be perfect by you?

When you settle, you give up a part of yourself, the self that would not normally accept some particular habits in a relationship. This is time for Elementary Thinking, taking the time to make better choices and live well, happy and in love.

Love can burn so brightly, its heat melts into your soul and will fuse someone special to it. This burn can also sting, leaving a wound that often will never heal.

When I was younger, I met a woman that I found a certain chemistry with and we began to date. We quickly progressed into intimacy, with frequent expressions of it. There is relationship drama to be found here and my young heart was just waiting to be negatively tested.

We very quickly became an item, and then became part of life on campus. We were at ease with each other intellectually and socialized as a couple often. It was very easy for the two of us to talk to each other and we were much more than sexually compatible.

The drama began when we both returned from summer vacation. Returning home, she no longer spoke to me. I was left without a reason for my emptiness, my loss. I never knew the real reason why my first love was gone. Finding the infamous closure, would have helped my young broken heart. I could have used Elementary Thinking here, realizing that I could love myself first and be o.k. Because I did not have the tools to survive this lost love, I wandered aimlessly for many years in relationships. Often I would look for validation, carrying on several relationships at time. This provided a level of safety for me, not having to worry about being alone.

Realizing that my repeated drama here is the lack of an explanation of the reasons for the breaking up without a reason, I gave in. I decided to surrender my pride and make things workable for me. I made a conscious choice to change my own mindset, rationalizing that love is a great risk and challenge to the soul. It's not a bet with an insurance wager against the love of others.

Always remember in love, it begins with self. How can you say that you love another if you are not willing to share it with the beautiful and precious you? In the examples I gave you, there was a loving reaction. This reaction was often dramatically negative, but with a potential positive spin. Proactive love is within you and with that foundation, that sight; you can be the real positive hub of your circle of life.

I could have written more about love here, maybe that will be the subject of my next book. I tried to give you enough about love to show how Elementary Thinking can be applied to love and maybe help lessen the blows that injure the heart. Love is so difficult of a topic and yet can be so personally rewarding. If I could only have one wish for mankind, I would find a synthesis of what love is or could be. I would put this love in a bottle or pill and distribute it to the masses for free. It would be a vaccination against heartbreak. Of course anything you ingest should be a choice, but love is also infectious.

Could civilization learn to love itself? I hope after reading this book, it will start one person at a time.

DRAMATIC WITH PRIDE

I would guess that if you are going to write a book about drama, you would be remiss if you did not talk about vanity. Dramatic results on a large and diverse scale from the need for greater self. All of this to look the best, to appear to be more than anyone else.

It is one thing to work hard, be in the lead and savor your victory. It is another to present yourself as the leader, but only in view and not in action or manner.

Persons who are direct and motivated to achieve are often perceived as having an attitude. This description is only to mask their envy. Be motivated and achieve, what you gain is respect earned.

Is that what foolish pride is?

Earlier in the book I spoke about a 'ghetto' joke... "You know you're ghetto if your rims are worth more than your car." This is exactly where I'm going here. Pride says appear more than you really are. What could you have done with the money spent on the rims anyway?

True respect and pride are abstract, not tangible. These are things not bought, but earned. I keep touching on the same concepts, but I can't hammer this point home enough. Vanity is a poison, a disease that erodes who you are. It takes away the ability for anyone to deal with you on a mature level and eventually it will bring you down.

Pride is also a curse as well. When you deny yourself or loved ones because you can't bring yourself to ask for help. That is foolish pride and often punishes others for your inability to surrender. Even in the face of an offer to help not solicited by you, you say no.

How can you in good conscience allow bad things to happen or continue to happen because of your vanity? How will you appear when shame and regret become your new friends? All because you were only thinking about how you would look, your pride.

The pride-vanity thing is how we got to the car rims earlier. Do you think that buying things outside of your means relates here? Expensive clothing, jewelry, cars, and eating out often, fancy liquor purchases and so on. You know of someone or even yourself, victims of the pride-vanity cancer.

So, are pride and or vanity dramatic? Elementary Thinking can easily apply as a filter, a map to read before you go down this twisting road. For the most part, this is all about being someone you are not or want someone to see. This is just not the real you.

Vanity has and will always play a great role in history. How many stories have we heard or have been taught about the leaders that fell prey to their own vanity. This vanity coupled with greed became a catalyst for their downfall. The stories are numerous, filled with fancy uniforms, palaces and special military units dedicated to themselves.

The real problem with dramatic pride here is getting caught up in your own power. This creates a need to show everyone that you are in charge. Often you are so busy showing off, that you don't see the people that you want to respect you and their needs. Also, you don't see your rivals who want your `greatness' and wealth for themselves.

National pride steeped in greed and or vanity happens here as well. During the Second World War, Germany was seduced by national pride which caused them to conquer weaker nearby states. Vain and full of the lust for greatness, this new national pride also, blinded the German public to the ethnic cleansing it conducted killing millions.

Alexander, Hannibal and The Romans all fell prey to national pride and the vain notion that they were beyond the possibility of failure due to overreaching national need. They all tried to conquer the world and felt their cultures were so better than the people they conquered. This pride-vanity meant that they could hold onto the land and make these weak people like themselves or slaves.

Empires based upon the flawed belief of superiority, pure pride and vanity. This blinded the conquerors to the amount of effort needed to maintain them...And this relates to Elementary Thinking, how?

It's about a grounded self and your ability to maintain that grounding. Only God can have successes without end and not have to worry about having backup, the supply lines of life. When you move forward too quickly without thought and consideration, you shorten your ability to take along the nourishment needed to maintain your gains and propel yourself further.

If you wanted to go on a car trip somewhere, wouldn't you fill the car up with fuel first? Sandwiches, refreshments, snacks, map? That's being proactive, knowing your objective, assessing a reasonable way to accomplish your goal and starting a plan into motion that will be successful. Pride says to leave that map at home or there's more than enough gas to make it. Drama comes when the patrol car comes up behind you parked at the side of road and the officer uses the radio to call you a wrecker.

In all of this common sense stuff we must not forget pride's synonyms...including one's 'face.' What is this? It's a human beings dignity and value of self. In ancient Japanese society, loss of face meant that you were to take your own life to regain your respect.

Fueled by pride, you would stab yourself in the abdomen with a short sword and disembowel yourself. How good does your corpse look as its being taken away? That's about as dramatic as I would ever want for myself.

Ever hear of the estranged lover that killed because he or she lost love? Their acts justified and described as if they could not have that love, neither would anyone else. How about the harassing phone calls, following your 'ex' now with a new lover? I know this is not healthy, but it just describes more examples of how pride blinds you to relationship loss and your ability to use Elementary Thinking.

Embarrassment is another form of pride loss, much more on the public side. This is pure negative perception of self. If you don't love self, how can you expect to gain? You will not gain respect and your psyche will suffer. Is asking for or being given help a loss of pride or embarrassment? Is allowing yourself to be embarrassed really a loss of respect or is it your need to act as if you are alright? What if you ignored this embarrassment and continued on with life, passing up the need to duel to reclaim your honor. I would bet and you should agree that the act of reclamation is way too dramatic. What you are left with after you act is probably more damaging to you overall, than what you would be left with if you just walked away.

Using pride as an excuse for bad behavior is fine, but the consequences are again usually worse than what you would have dealt with originally. I don't need to tell you that when you retaliate, the person who originally offended you gets twice the benefit. They got to hurt you and you lash out, probably damaging yourself in the process. Elementary Thinking needs to stop this cycle of you did me, so now I do you mentality.

By the way, don't confuse pride with being macho or machismo. Trying to suppress your feelings because it might make you look weak? What if you actually showed your inner self to someone and took a risk? In some cultures you lose face if you give in to your feelings and tears are droplets of shame. Of course those macho or machismo rules apply here, so men can't cry. Women, you must be able to compete past stereotypes, so don't show your feelings. So, I wonder if all of this suppression of feelings in the name of pride could be stressful? Isn't pride supposed to be good, you know, to be proud for whatever reason?

Being self-destructive in the name of pride is a great sin. Why is it so difficult to ask for help? Often, the consequences of what you are not asking help about are so great and lead to so much personal and business drama. Sometimes for things so small, a risk needs to be taken.

What am I talking about?

You can never really know anger until you deal with neglect of the elderly. Remember your parent or relative living away from you or in a nursing facility. Remind yourself that when your body grows old, your mind may not. So, now your mind is trapped in a body that will not respond to your desires. Pride says do not ask for help, so you will survive, right? Live out your fantasies of lost youth as you self-medicate with alcohol or drugs.

With a limited and fixed income, the elderly are faced with hard choices. Basic nutritional needs are often met in very basic ways. Protein is found cheaply in the pet food isle while shopping and other basic needs like warmth are left behind in the monthly budget.

Denial with a need for self-sufficiency can help in the creation of the best stories of the good life shared by all. As human beings we live with a core belief that we control our own individual destiny and are truly proud of the amount of so called wealth we each can accumulate. Limit this ability and `the train comes off of the tracks.' Pride in your ability to provide for loved ones says to give money, even though your own bills are not paid. Give food, even though your own pantry is empty. Serious illnesses will be hidden or denied as not to `burden' anyone.

Pay close attention to the elderly in your lives; allow Elementary Thinking to override the need for privacy here. This is the one point where you may need to become forceful to gain that positive result. Looking at the big picture here, you can see that intervention can provide healing for all and a strengthening or bonding. Don't forget that in some cases, these were people that assumed the role of mentor in your youth. And now, it is you that must become the caregiver. You won't be seen as that good kid they remember, just some disrespectful person who should mind their own business. Frustration can also kick pride up another notch too. Don't even think that until you explain or otherwise reason with someone, they will deny their pride and accept help blindly.

Can pride mask your ability to detect need? Can pride mask the realization that love has a greater healing power than any drug, doctor or financial transaction? Is pride in human terms really just another word for control, or a tool of manipulation?

Someone insults another and the fists fly. Of course, pride demands a response here and not the human nature excuse. So, violence is most often the result of being prideful for some self-serving purpose or you just being on the receiving end of its negative expression by someone else.

Don't allow your pride to get in the way of other people's feelings or get the best of yours. To feel good about self and accomplishments is a good thing. Pride requires a great balancing act between emotion and self-preservation. Elementary Thinking makes a great focal point here, but don't expect it from others.

So, let's sum up. We know that true respect and pride are abstract, not tangible. Respect and pride cannot be bought, only earned. It is one thing to work hard and savor your victory as you lead. It is another to present you as the leader, but only in view and not in action or manner. Want for pride can bring you so far out of self to a fault. Living beyond your means can come easy as a result of foolish pride. Sometimes allowing another to save face will cost you less than the cost of their negative emotions. Pride will mask your ability to detect need, be open minded and watchful. Pride transcends age, so remember the elderly. Treat them as if they soon will be you.

Pride really can be more negative and less of value than you think. All the energy you use can be amplified in the envy response to your intention. So, don't be the person who gets caught not walking the talk.

A DRAMATIC RETURN

As we travel, we must deal with many trials and tests which can alter our direction to our final destination. I know trials and tests is a really lousy metaphor, but the reality comes here in what I have to say.

Often we as fallible human beings can make simple mistakes, minor spills on the floor of life. But, for some the cyclic nature of life is something that can't be fixed with anything that we could buy, ask for or make.

Drama can return as fast as lightning and can leave you wondering about the results of your hard cleansing work. What do I mean here? I am speaking of trying to lead a good life, right?

Let me begin with choices we make as young people. Our parents have a responsibility to provide us with the proper mind set to survive and thrive. Animals do it and humans should too. So, I guess a little guidance wouldn't hurt here. A map of life is not readily available, but experience can be a great teacher. I would sure hope that your own trial and error could really be a great help to a loved one, right? How about something as simple as telling someone that this is how it works and this happens when you don't do it right.

A young mind is like a new sponge, fresh and ready to absorb anything. As parents and loved ones, our thoughts are liquid and should be poured slowly and deliberately for the greatest absorption. I hate to use the canvas metaphor here, but here goes.

A young and new life is a blank canvas waiting for the color and texture of experiences. The duty here is to provide the best start, a beginning to travel down a better path to success and maybe even more. Close personal interaction with our children, a bonding that can hold a lifetime together. Love and support with the connection of thought, conversation, physical activity and nutrition. But, most of all, just some high quality time together.

Unfortunately, there are some who believe that as adults they should live out their own lost youth in their children. Instead of providing an environment of growth, a heavy blanket of self-pity weighs down any opportunity of self-discovery. In other words, the grown up who hasn't grown up, is blocking their own child's ability to mature.

I know you have seen this before, the old making up for lost time syndrome. Oh, but I digress. Anyway, parents set the course their children take and then maturing, learn the path and continue on.

Humans and animals, it has worked the same way since the beginning of time.

Can you smell the aroma of drama here yet? Earlier, I spoke about how Elementary Thinking does not exist in the young, it's developed. This might explain why in most states you can have a juvenile criminal record that remains sealed as you become a legal adult. If you are not mature enough or have any guidance, why should you be saddled with a mark against your name for life?

So, where does drama fit in here? As you grow older, you are allowed to make choices for yourself by default. Often, just leaving home for school is the opening for drama. Mommy and daddy are not there for kids once they leave the nest for a day's education. Throughout the day, young people have to make choices, some good and some life altering. We have all heard the tragic stories, the excessive or binge drinking. The terrible car crashes, drug abuse, senseless violence, suicide and teen pregnancy.

When you make a bad choice in your youth, you can expect a return on your negative investment. As you grow older and try to reach out and grab your dreams, it just seems that so much is just out of your grasp. You keep reaching out, but it moves with you. You move, it moves. It keeps a perfect distance, just a small frustrating distance away. Another way of considering this is, think of the four tires on a car. When the car starts to move, all of the wheels turn at the same rate and so when slowing to a stop. Round, wheel, cyclic, drama?

So, I guess I'm rambling on. What I really need to do is explain how the things we talked about earlier, come back around and shape the now and things to come. Come back around, like in a circle?

In Chapter Four, we talked about being able to detect dramatic events before they caused us harm. If you really can't see whats coming, it hits you and sets you off the course you want to take for success. Your end comes without reaching your goals, all because you weren't ready to go forward with eyes open.

In Chapter Seven we discussed being more than we really are or embellishing on our pedigree. How can you succeed if the foundation of which you travel from is weak or tainted by falsehoods? Let people see the real you, it doesn't require later explanation. There is nothing worse than being undermined by not being able to walk the talk. Of course the real handicap is your inability to actually be qualified to be what you say. There, I said it enough ways for you to understand.

In Chapter Eight, The Drama of Sex, it again was all about choices and their consequences. Not being protected is a big thing here. Would you subject another if you contracted an S.T.D? So, how about your legacy? You know, the ability to meet a new partner and have a baby. Future not so bright sexually. Making a bad choice which can keep haunting you and others, cyclic?

Chapter Ten had us discussing the many reasons why we should take better care of ourselves. You know, taking care of self is better than having loved ones take care of you or your affairs. Not taking care of you now and paying later. Family members can also now be caught up in your choices, even in your demise. Funeral costs, unsecured loans of yours or just plain fixing your debt. It is even worse when you become ill and need long-term care because of decisions that you made, selfish ones. Now, family members have their lives altered along with yours taking care of you. So watching your diet and getting off of your butt might not be a bad thing.

The Price of Drama in Chapter Eleven is your not being able to take care of your own financial messes and sometimes leaving it to loved ones. Of course financial stress would not lead to illness, right? So, that extra pair of shoes you couldn't afford, which gave you more bills...More bills which gave you stress and led to your hypertension and your diabetes, then a stroke and premature death.

Sounds like it all comes back around as a vicious circle of bad choices. Cyclic? By the way, who or how many really pay the price?

In Drama By Misdirection, it was about being accountable for self and not providing your opinion of others accountability. When did you develop a level of perfection to set the standard for others to follow? Oh man, it's that spiritual bible stuff again. You know, doing unto others, casting the first stone, etc. Still, minding your own business is the generic version of what we're really talking about. That person that you outed or rumormongered about once upon a time, might be pivotal in your future somehow. Wouldn't it be unfortunate if that person was later involved in your promotion and or retention during budget cuts. What if your misdirection led to someone feeling so much despair that they took their own life? Is that drama and would it haunt you, following you around like a shadow? Be responsible for self and be positive for others. A positive environment can nurture all in it including you.

Dramatic With Pride, Chapter Sixteen. The smallest of things could mean so much to so many. Yet the usual amount of kindness by the wealthy is the foundation with their name on it and used to soften their tax burden as a write off. My fantasy is to be wealthy enough to be able to take some daily interest and give away prepaid debit cards to strangers. That would be my new day job. No notoriety, anonymous gifts at shelters and churches. Gifts to every day people to brighten a day. In the employment line, at the Social Services lobby. Pride also says take the offered gift and heal, you can return the gift when things are better.

This may sound sappy, but look at the truth in it...A life filled with service can be rewarding on it's own. It doesn't have to be acknowledged for that ego thing, just done because it's the right thing to do. The cycle here is that even the tangible reward doesn't have to be there for you to win. The pride you can have is service and a job well done. Don't expect reward, it makes reward all the more sweeter when it happens.

Courage can play a large role in the life experience. Each of us must draw upon it from the stores within self. Does waking and getting out of bed qualify? What about that extra food or drink? Do you think the consequences of our excesses will not follow us around? The things that some of us take for granted, the small steps through daily life, can be mountains for others.

Do you remember that cup of positive outlook? This is how we get through our days. Sometimes, all we have is a smile. But, a smile can open a closed and locked door. This power can sometimes insulate you from past drama either directly or indirectly. Directly by changing perception or focus. Indirectly by allowing you to love yourself again. Warning, the direction can be altered by your own cyclic travel and how negative your past journey was. Folks, some transgressions are way beyond the ability for others to forgive. So, along with Elementary Thinking you need to add a spoonful of common sense.

I have always looked in wonder at my life and choices. You always talk about the what if and if I only did this or that. I wrote this book about the start of my journey and my route of travel. My personal lessons are a map which I drew on it's pages. I had to learn the hard way, as we all do. In any journey, we must remain positive, the best alternative.

Each and every day, I try to apply the principles of which I speak. Elementary Thinking is the thing which provides me with the tools to survive and the ability to see ahead. It is truly the way to navigate forward and weave backward. It is not a cure for the past, but it sure can help in a pinch.

As I look back, I wonder about the past and theories regarding time travel or just wishes to transport self. I don't regret my beautiful children or some of the other inspired choices I made in life. But I have to wonder about the power of Elementary Thinking and that one changed element away from controversy. Where would I be now and who would I have become?

I am thankful for life and my experiences, I am rich in many ways. Thankfulness is a wealth of good spirit, outlook and love. This cocktail is the only one you can abuse and benefit. The wealth you can have, but never spend all of. Even when you think too much has passed earthly for you to find redemption, remember there was at least one thing somewhere. You had to have done something right and important, if not for someone, it was for your yourself. That means that there is good in you and over a period of time an accumulation of worth. That's the wealth I speak of and the basis for remembering no life is wasted and a new beginning is around every corner.

Every person who has ever passed this way is at least one or more steps from bottom. Bottom is the womb, our birth is the beginning. If someone smiled because they saw you as an infant, you gave them a happy thought. That's one step from bottom and a lift from the beginning. I know all of this sounds too simplistic, but why does the little things in life have to be complicated?

So, even when drama comes back around or never leaves your side, a healing way is within us all. Some transgressions cannot be left behind, but there can be a new start just a moment away.

I just wanted to touch base on some old themes, that cyclic thing. So, I guess this is starting to sound like the same old song and like I am talking in circles. The cyclic significance is very relative.

So be it.

EPILOGUE

So here we are. You know about Elementary Thinking and drama. I have given you too many examples of dramatic fire starters and just pure controversy. I floated in some of my opinion to stir conversation, the overall premise of this book. I hope using Elementary Thinking, you can find some peace in a chaotic world.

This book is about healing with and through personal lines of communication. It's about looking ahead and not running into obstacles while looking behind. It's about remembering to take each and every day, give it a goal and treating it like it was going to be your last.

So many examples of drama and some seemed repetitious I'm sure. But, you have to realize that drama is cyclic and if you don't break the cycle, it will come back around to visit you again and again. On the return trip it may take another form, a variation of the first dramatic controversy. Just as painful and just as damaging.

Elementary Thinking is not really a new concept; I told you that the good books talk about it. But, what is new is that everyone is included in the circle of life, no exceptions. No intolerance of other thought and the sharing of the abundance that is you with your circle and the world.

As I close this book, I think back to the first thoughts of its creation and the many months of self-discovery while writing it. Discovering that I had so much inside waiting to spill out onto paper, the spillage, healing as well as giving. The many months of writing, at all times of the day and night. The edit and further discovery about myself and this work.

It was very hard to give some of the examples seen literally through my own eyes and the eyes of those I have known and loved. I put our pain on some of the previous pages and wrote the text with our tears. Some of the images are ugly, some make you want to laugh at how you got there too.

Remember from the very beginning, I told you I was not a doctor. I also said that I do not make any clinical claims. I decided to share with you a new way of thinking, taking you along my own journey of personal discovery. A discovery of a new way of living, being yourself and being open to others as they struggle through each and every day too.

There are no references to the works of others here. These are my thoughts, my concepts and I will answer for them if need be. I refuse to judge, so I offer situations and a remedy which I gave birth to on the preceding pages. This book was neither medical journal nor fairy tale. It is about an ordinary person, talking to ordinary people about the way ordinary people live and love life.

If you didn't understand what I was writing about, I hope that at least you will talk about what you read. You can still use this as a catalyst for conversation, and that's not really so bad. What would be unfortunate is to see anyone look at this work and just shrug their shoulders.

I just ask that you think about these concepts I laid out and see if any of the examples of drama I gave relate to you. No matter where or how you live, there is drama and this drama is larger than you or your life.

This book is really about the human brain, the ultimate drama factory and hospital. You either self-empower and heal, deflect what comes next or make more drama by closing down your intellect. Stop thinking and lose control of your drama as it comes, start thinking and learn to heal thyself.

In our new thinking, we practice forgiveness, and early intervention or being proactive as an effort to self-empower. We set daily goals, surrendering and realizing that we are only human. We now take responsibility for what we do, learn from it and avoid its return.

This new proactive thinking says it takes more time to repair mistakes when rushing to completion, than it would if you took time to focus straight ahead and travel slowly initially. Straight and smooth, maybe even with a new sense of purpose. Travel with a new awareness of how you want to live and to love, self-empowered and strong.

Now that you have read this, I hope that you can find your way to the light at the end of your own tunnel. Be forever proactive as you journey. You don't have to forget where you came from, just don't look back. Look ahead without blinders on, no tunnel vision. Keep the Circle of Life diagram in your memory and remember that what you do or the decisions you make can effect so many.

A little common sense can go a long way.

Remember, you can limit the drama, by eliminating the elements of controversy.

CPSIA information can be obtained at www.ICGtesting.com
Printed in the USA
BVOW040319010313

314503BV00001B/23/P